RAGGY

ARSED

LADS™

ALLAN FINLAY

RAGGY ARSED LADS

Although based on a true story, this novel is entirely a work of fiction.
The names and characters portrayed in this book are the work
of the author's imagination. Any resemblance to actual persons,
living or dead, events or localities, is entirely coincidental.

Allan Finlay asserts the moral right to
be identified as the author of this work, in accordance
with the Copyright, Designs and Patents Act, 1988.

ISBN: 978-1-906722-35-7

For my boys-
Henry and George.

Acknowledgements

I would like to thank many people who have, over the
years, shared their stories with me, and to those who have influenced
the funny situations I often find myself in.

Some of the original 'Raggy Arsed Lads' I grew up with;
John Swift, Albert and Kevin Smith, Rusty Salmon, Walter Hesslewood,
Cyril Hodgson, Roy Armstrong, Trevor Wigley, The Thorntons,
Graham Barratt, Jonny Johnston, Brian Larner, Two Foot, Stuart Melrose,
John Corbett, Alan Wyatt, Ken Hadfield and the rest, especially my father.

Thank you to Vincent Edgar, Sue McKay, Jonathan Power, Tony Frearson and Dave Norton
for being the first to read this book, and for their kind and constructive criticism.

Facebook- /RaggyArsedLads

Twitter- @RaggyArsedLads

Preface

After World War II, England's nationalised industries expanded; they gave work to the thousands who were desperate to feed their families. In the North of England the choice one had was governed mainly by the industry that was particular to the region, generally the woollen mills, the paper mills, the brick or glass works and the coal mines. The choice of job also had a lot to do with family pride: for example, if your father was a coal miner and his father before him, then you should be honoured to follow in their footsteps. If it was good enough for them, it should be good enough for you.

Other opportunities were few and far between. If one came your way you were soon talked out of it. Generally speaking I think this was because of two reasons; the first was if you went to work somewhere else, they'd miss you. The second was because nobody wanted you to better yourself. It was often easier to be stuck in a rut, for this way there was at least some sort of sense of security and you knew that you were guaranteed to get something at the end of the week to pay the rent.

The hardship of the nationalised industries cemented the comradeship of the workers. They lived for the moment when all else failed and they were at rock bottom; their strong characters would allow them to take the Michael out of themselves and others. Laughter was sometimes the cure, although occasionally it made matters worse, but more often than not, the laughter worked out to be the best solution. For example, if someone lay in the gutter, homeless with no clothes on their back and feeling sorry for themselves, you would expect someone to go up to him and say, 'Come on, let me help you', and then do their best to get them up onto their feet and back on the right track. If a Raggy Arsed Lad saw a poor soul laying in the gutter, they would walk up to them and instead say, 'Get up you daft bastard!'. It's not that they didn't care; it's just that they had a funny way of showing it. In fact, they probably cared more than most.

The class system at the time suppressed the depressed. By keeping the working class poor, meant the rich had no competition, less cars on the road and exclusivity to expensive things and venues. Many insecure inherited-wealth millionaires enjoyed the security that if a self-made man did come into their realm it would be an extremely rare occurrence.

Based on a true story…

1
At the Beginning

Well, where do I start? It was a long time ago, that's for sure, in a little smoky mining town up north. The thick smog filled the air first thing in a morning. At that time you could see the miners and brick workers coming and going, changing shifts. The ones covered in soot or clay were those going home and those still covered in soot or clay were the ones returning to work.

The town was quite hilly and sat surrounded by beautiful countryside. There was always something happening; kids chasing each other down the streets, folks running here, there and everywhere doing their shopping, getting their fresh bread first thing in a morning from the bakers, a pound or so of stewing meat from the butcher or fresh grown vegetables from someone else's allotment. The paperboys would be out, each with their own route, and then back home in time to get ready for school. Rows of stone and brick terraced houses ran in all directions to and from the town, all with little smoking chimneys on their roof's ridge. Most of the houses were spotless and well maintained with a sense of pride, the scoured clean front steps and the variously coloured front doors glistening in the sun.

The pits were the main industry in the town. You must have heard the stories; when a boy left school at the age of sixteen, his father would take him down to the pit office for a job and that was that. There was not much choice otherwise. The pits were their best bet and the way the townspeople thought, why shouldn't it be? The pits had become an institution. The managers were hard with their workers, but having said that, they looked after their own. A job at the coalface was hard, cold and wet, but nobody moaned, they just got on with the job. It was an occupation these men felt they were lucky to have and they were proud and glad of it.

Those who didn't work at the pit were the ones who went against the grain. They were looked upon as someone who wouldn't have been able to hack it down the mine. After all, the miners had one of the hardest jobs in the world - they worked hard, played hard and were steadfast together. They were a great bunch when you got to know them, but then, you had to get to know them and before you could do that, they had to like you.

*

Tommy McCue was a strapping lad, who no doubt could have coped with life down the pit. Therefore, the taunts from the odd miner didn't bother him. His father had been a miner and was tragically killed in a mine collapse when Tommy was only fifteen, leaving the youngster to get the odd job here and there to help support his mother. Tommy was a clever lad, who had done well at school. He would probably have gone on to higher education if his father hadn't been killed. He was a good-looking chap, just under six foot tall with short, dark wavy hair, a light complexion and blue eyes. You could tell by his physique that Tommy was a fighter, a lad who could look after himself, although you would never hear him mentioning it. His aspiration was to make something of himself and he wasn't scared of hard work. Tommy liked a laugh and was a bit of a joker, but when things got tough, so would Tommy McCue.

By the time Tommy was in his mid-twenties, he had built on the small amount of compensation awarded to his mother for the death of her husband. He owned a small yard in the town just on the bend of Stumble Street, where three terraced houses had once stood. The adjoining end of the remaining row of houses showed the remains of a fireplace and chimney stack overlooking the yard. You could still see from the yard side what was left of the wallpaper hanging from what was now an external wall. Around the front of the yard was a small stone wall that ran up to the entrance gates, which had been made from many pieces of reclaimed metal fabricated together.

Upstairs in the end terrace that accompanied the yard was Tommy's office where Rosie worked. The downstairs was just a store, filled with lots of greasy old engine parts. The next house down was a hairdresser-cum-barber's shop.

Rosie was Tommy's secretary and had retired from the pit office some years previously. She was small and fiery; she spoke her mind and took no crap from anyone, especially when sticking up for Tommy.

The sign on the yard said:

THOMAS McCUE
Non-Ferrous Metals and Demolition

His main business in reality was taking down old air raid shelters, keeping the metal sheets for scrap and selling them on to the scrap dealers. If, however, any other opportunities came along to make a bob or two he'd jump at it; like house clearances or dismantling and scrapping old vehicles, saving and selling the parts or trying to sell an old car, for instance, from the 'forecourt' of his yard.

Big Barry was Tommy's right-hand man; he was in his late twenties, stood about six foot five and probably weighed around twenty-five stone. He had curly mousy-coloured hair down to his collar and black grease engrained into his hands and fingers. He could never get a pair of overalls to fit him. Every time you saw Barry you couldn't help but notice a gap between the bottom of his shirt and the top of his trousers, which unfortunately meant the bottom of his beer gut and the top of his arse were always hanging out. It was obvious Barry wouldn't have survived down the mines - he was a gentle giant. That's one of the reasons why Tommy had taken Big Barry under his wing. However, Barry was a bloody good mechanic, he was as strong as an ox and he could fart for England.

With Big Barry on board, the little business could mend and service cars and the like, but it was a business on a constant uphill struggle, barely keeping its head above water.

*

Tommy had a little car for sale on the front of his yard, an old Austin 10, and that morning a middle-aged man had come through the gates and was looking at the car.

"Morning," Tommy said as he approached the man.

"How much is the car?" was the reply.

"How much have you got?" came the answer.

"Ten pounds is all I have," said the man.

"*Ten pounds*? You can't buy a car for just ten pounds! What do you think this is, a charity shop? I'll tell you what, give me fifty pounds and she's all yours."

"Not bloody likely," said the man, "I'll give you twenty."

"Twenty, I thought you only had ten?"

The man continued around the car kicking all four of its tyres. Tommy thought to himself how he could really do with the twenty pounds, but having been in similar situations before, he knew he should not choose the easy option and take the money. Therefore, discipline was needed and he should hold out for the full price.

"I'll tell you what," said Tommy. "Forty pounds and I'll throw in a full tank of petrol."

The discipline had turned to desperation.

"I'll think about it," the man said as he walked out of the yard.

"What's there to think about? Think of what you'll save on bus fares," Tommy said as he followed him out.

"I'll think about it!" and off the man went.

Tommy sighed and looked down, nothing was ever easy.

*

Like I said, the main job of the business was collecting old air raid shelter sheets from wherever they could. Tommy would put little line adverts in newspapers; one time for example, a letter from Lincolnshire from a Mrs Britches had arrived requiring the services of Tommy to 'remove the eyesore in her garden'.

Rosie had arranged the appointment time, and later that week Tommy, Barry and a young lad called Norman set off to Mablethorpe in their old Bedford flatback lorry. It blew smoke out all the way there; it looked a bit odd seeing such a filthy thing driving through the beautiful Lincolnshire countryside, past several of the old overgrown abandoned airfields of World War II.

There were only two seats in the lorry, so Young Norman had to sit cross-legged in the middle on top of the engine compartment, but he didn't mind, he was just thrilled to be there.

The villagers were out in the fields helping the farmers to bring in the harvest. The old threshing machines were at work and the haystacks were growing in number.

It was about lunchtime when they hit Mablethorpe and pulled over for something to eat.

"Pass the snap box, Norman," said Tommy.

Norman looked nervous and gave a slight smile.

"You've forgotten the bloody snap, haven't you?"

Norman again looked nervous and gave a slight smile.

"I gave you it and you put it on the desk in the office, I said make sure you don't forget our lunch."

There was no answer from Norman - just a slight smile.

Barry suggested calling at a chip shop, but none of them had any money.

"Bollocks!"

Off they went to get the job done, so they could get paid as soon as possible and get something to eat.

After driving around Mablethorpe for half an hour, they finally found the street on the address Rosie had given them and then they looked for the house number.

"Here it is," said Norman.

They backed the lorry up the drive of a rather nice detached brick house with a holly bush on the front lawn. The garden was a little overgrown. Tommy got out, knocked on the door and an old lady answered.

"Come in, come in," she said.

"Mrs Britches?" Tommy enquired.

"Come in, you look famished. Would you and your men like some tea and home-made cakes before you start?" she asked.

"That would be lovely, Mrs Britches, but let us remove the shelter and load it up first then we would love to sample your cooking... Although a couple of sandwiches wouldn't go amiss, to get us started!"

Tommy felt an instant liking for Mrs Britches. She was an old war widow and it was clear Tommy had taken pity on her.

Tommy handed Barry and Norman a sandwich and then the team quickly set about dismantling the old air raid shelter in the rear of the garden. With his arse on show, Big Barry stood bent over on the roof with his burning gun, cutting through the bolts that held the sheets together. One by one the sheets came free and Norman carried them to the lorry. Tommy swung his fourteen-pound hammer at the concrete and brick base, then shovelled the rubble up into bags to take away to sell as hardcore. Once the shelter sheets were loaded, Tommy had Norman cut the grass for the old lady, while he swept up around the house and Barry trimmed the holly bush on the front garden.

Mrs Britches couldn't thank them enough - it had been a long time since she'd had her bush trimmed, so she got out her best china and poured the tea and handed out her home-made cakes. Needless to say there were none left by the time they left. A good deal, and a good deed done - a satisfying combination.

Of course a trip to the seaside wouldn't be complete without seeing the sea and now, with a little money in his pocket, Tommy headed for a fish shop on the front. As nice as they were, Mrs Britches' home-made cakes weren't enough to fill those three, so it was fish, chips and peas, three times, with salt and vinegar, open in newspaper and eaten by the sea.

2

Back Then

Tommy McCue was born and bred in the town; he grew up in a poor but happy family environment. On their street the kids would play football after school almost every night and they would also get up to all the antics that most kids got up to. He was a popular member of his class and throughout the school, and was top at most subjects, but most of all he lived for his football. Tommy was centre forward for the school team.

He stayed out of trouble most of the time, apart from when he thought it would be really funny to light the communal bonfire in the local park the day before it was due to go up. The bonfire was massive; the council had been building it for weeks with all sorts of things from wooden pallets to old rafters and sofas. Many of the locals had helped by getting rid of some old things that needed burning, others would help by taking some wood home to burn it on their own fires in their front room. Tommy thought it would be funny to set it going the night before. He was only twelve and I don't think he realised the enormity of the prank. The bonfire went up like a forest fire and within minutes the fire brigade had been called, a crowd had gathered and a big red fire engine had arrived.

The firemen put the fire out with their hoses and saved most of the bonfire for the following night, but when the town mayor tried to light it he couldn't because the wood was wet through.

Tommy kept stum about the whole thing, but somehow he was labelled as the kid who ruined bonfire night that year, but as nobody saw him do it and he never admitted it, he was never reprimanded. His dad always stuck up for him. When asked if their Tommy lit the fire, he'd answer:

"Did he bloody hellers like."

Tommy's dad was called Martin; he was the spitting image of what Tommy would grow into. Martin was popular around the town and at the pit, and was well known for his funny 'but true' stories. He was a family man at heart and a good provider to his son and his wife, whom he loved dearly. He and his wife had been together since they were sixteen, they were married at twenty and Tommy arrived eight months later.

Their house was an end of terrace, with a well kept old dining room table in the bay window of their front room, which also had an open fire. The rest of the house was adorned with well made second-hand, hand-me-down furniture that would today look expensive and antique, but back then it just looked old and second hand. However, the sideboard, the side cabinet and the table shone with polish and elbow wax. You could set your watch by the grandfather clock in the entrance hall. In the back was the kitchen with its little white stove and a small kitchen table with three chairs. Upstairs were the bedroom of course and outside there was a small walled backyard.

Martin and Tommy's father-and-son relationship was probably the best you would ever find. Martin, when he wasn't working, would often join in the football on the street or he would go and stand on the touchline and watch Tommy play in matches whenever he could. Martin would often go for walks, taking Tommy with him, mainly to the park where he would try to build into Tommy a sense of ambition in the hope he would not be enticed to follow everyone else, but be independent and stand on his own two feet. He wanted Tommy to achieve all the things in life that he should have, not like himself who had followed the crowd - to the pit office. However, when Martin had his friends and workmates around him, he would never mention anything about going it alone.

One time Tommy asked his dad about the talks they had had in front of his pit colleagues and Martin ashamedly pretended he didn't know what his son was talking about, but Tommy had an old head on his young shoulders and he knew it was pride that made his dad act that way.

*

The day Martin was killed was dreadful. It knocked the whole town sideways. A tunnel in the mine had started to collapse and all but two had made it out. Martin thought he knew where the two men had been working and ran back in to bring them out, but it wasn't to be. No sooner had he entered the danger area when the tunnel completely collapsed, killing him and the other two.

The miners pulled together for the bereaved families. Several of them visited Mrs McCue to tell her the bad news. She was outside in their backyard hanging out the washing when they told her; she sobbed uncontrollably as they took her inside and sat her down. One of Martin's workmates went to get his wife to come and stay with Mrs McCue for that evening.

Poor Mrs McCue was in a terrible state.

"What about Tommy?" she kept shouting.

Tommy was at school. One of the miners, a chap called Bert, who was a good friend of Martins, said he would go and tell Tommy. He left the house with the burden of the responsibility.

Bert walked up to the school trembling, but trying not to show his emotion so he could be strong for Tommy. He walked through the main entrance of the school to the headmaster's office and knocked on the door. The headmaster opened the door and invited Bert in.

Bert told him the sad news and then said:

"I think I should be the one to tell Tommy."

The headmaster agreed and walked Bert to Tommy's classroom. As the headmaster entered the room, the class rose to their feet. He asked the class teacher if Tommy McCue could be excused. The teacher nodded, Tommy left his desk and went to the headmaster who said:

"There is someone here to see you."

Tommy looked at Bert, who tried to give the lad a smile and then put his hand on Tommy's shoulder.

"Come on, Tommy, lad, let's take a walk outside and onto the playing fields."

Tommy looked a little bewildered and confused as Bert walked him away from the school buildings.

"I have some terrible news Tommy; it's about your dad. There's been a pit collapse and he was caught up in it."

Bert was trying to find the words.

"Is he okay?" Tommy asked in hope.

"No, Tommy, lad, I'm afraid not. He died trying to save some of the others. You should be very proud of him."

The headmaster stood with his arms behind his back, looking on from his office window, out onto the playing fields, and saw young Tommy fall sobbing to his knees. He could see Bert was doing his best trying to hold it together - this chap who had come to bear the bad news had no easy task.

Bert knew young Tommy was a tough character, as he tried to hide his face so Bert wouldn't see his tears.

"There's no shame in crying, lad," Bert said. "Let those emotions out. This is something that you will never get over, but as time goes by you will learn to live with it and be able to control the pain."

Tommy had to wait for the sobbing to ease before he could get his words out.

"I d-don't know what to d-do."

Bert took hold of Tommy by the arms and stood him up.

"Now listen to me, Tommy McCue. I'll tell you what you should do now. You should stay away from that road to despair, get yourself sorted out because you are the man of the house now and you have your mother to look after. Tommy, now it is your turn to shine in life, so make your dad proud in whatever you do, he'll be looking down on you. You have your whole life ahead of you. I know you were brought up with a level head, lad, now it's time to use it."

Tommy took a deep breath and nodded to Bert.

"I need to go home," he said and off he ran.

*

At the house Mrs McCue was sitting in the kitchen where a lot of her friends had gathered, offering their condolences. The grandfather clock in the hall had stopped and there was an air of silence.

Tommy ran through the doorway shouting for his mother.

"It's Tommy," she said, "Tommy, I'm in here!"

Tommy ran to his mother and they embraced; it was a warm but sad sight to see. All they had now was each other.

*

Just about the whole town turned out for the funeral. It was a joint funeral for the three who were killed, for which the colliery had paid. Horse-drawn carriages transported the coffins up to St Mary's Church while the families walked behind. Tommy held his mother's arm as they walked.

"Tommy," she said, "I want you to promise me you will never take a job at the pit."

Tommy thought long and hard before he gave his answer, because he felt somehow a promise made today, to his mother, at his father's funeral, could never be broken. He wanted to think about it longer, but couldn't.

"I promise," he said.

*

The months that followed were hard. There was no money coming into the McCue's house at all. However, the miners would leave things on the doorstep of the house. This was done anonymously as the miners found it hard to show their emotions or their generosity, they just wanted to do their bit. Mrs McCue or Tommy would often open the door to find a carton of cream or some freshly caught trout from the river, which had been wrapped in newspaper and left on the step, or a brace of partridge hung on the door handle. The local poachers were very generous with other folks' stuff.

*

Tommy finished his last year at school and at sixteen left to find a job. However, the only one available was that of a miner and it was offered straight to him, but when he turned it down it caused a little animosity. The poachers stopped calling, all except the one who brought the fish, nobody could have told him to stop delivering.

Tommy would go out all hours. He had a couple of gardening and window cleaning jobs through the week, but he spent most of his time collecting bits of metal to weigh in. He would store things in the backyard of their house and slowly, over the next year or so, started to make a little money out of it.

*

Eighteen months or so later, Mrs McCue was given the five hundred pounds compensation for the death of her husband, and with that she bought a little yard on Stubble Street for Tommy.

"Are you daft, Mum?" Tommy asked at the time, and seemed quite annoyed with his mother. "You could buy other things with that money, things we need. I don't need another yard; I've got our backyard to store my stuff."

Nevertheless, the deal was done and Tommy moved his scrap business to Stumble Street.

*

The first few years on Stumble Street were very hard and Tommy was exposed to the nosey onlookers who frequently passed his yard. He often noticed the miners and others going out to the pubs and clubs usually when he was walking home from his yard on his way to a night in, because he didn't have enough money to spend on going out. He often thought about the promise that he had made his mother and wondered if maybe he shouldn't have made it, but he had and that was that. Tommy would never break a promise anyway, never mind one he had made to his mother. So back then, at that time, he would have to make do, working all hours collecting and selling scrap metal.

3

The Uphill Struggle

The town council resided in the town hall at the top of the hill, not far from Tommy's yard on Stumble Street. Most of the councillors at the time were 'jobsworths' and Cllr Bumsgrove was about the worst. He was a slightly built small man in his mid-thirties, whose job gave him a little bit of power; power to dictate to and control the ordinary person, power without responsibility.

They say that Cllr Bumsgrove had the piss taken out of him for most of his life. This had turned him into a very bitter man, hell-bent on taking it out on society. Some say he'd been bummed; we will never know. He had a special dislike for anyone trying to make something of themselves, probably due to him knowing that he would never better the job or the station in life that he himself held.

Cllr William Pollock was Cllr Bumsgrove's boss. William, or Bill to his friends, was head of the council and also the town mayor. Cllr Pollock was in his late fifties, an ex-manager of the pit and on most committees in the town, his favourite post being that of chairman to the committee of The Shaft Working Men's Club. Cllr Pollock was also very proud to hold the position of chief magistrate within the town's local court. It's fair to say he was a pompous old sod, with the biggest beer belly you have ever seen, but apparently under all that front and the walrus moustache, he wasn't too bad a fellow.

It was a Thursday when the paths of Cllr Bumsgrove and Tommy McCue crossed. The councillor was on his way to investigate a complaint he had received, regarding the hairdresser's shop on Stumble Street developing a strong smell of urine.

On his way to the hairdresser's shop Cllr Bumsgrove noticed a stream of black smoke. As he rounded the corner, it was clear it was coming from Tommy's yard. The councillor entered the yard as Big Barry came around a small van that was in the yard having the tyres changed. Barry was carrying a large gas tank under his left arm and a big oxygen bottle on his right shoulder.

Cllr Bumsgrove started shouting at Barry.

"You can't just burn tyres like that and smoke out the area. It's

 just diabolical!"

"Do you have an appointment?" Big Barry enquired politely.

"No, I do not!" was the councillor's answer.

"Well, piss off then!" said Barry, with a big smile on his face.

Once Big Barry started to laugh he couldn't stop and it wasn't long before he had to put the heavy cylinders down before he dropped them. Barry had meant no harm in what he had just said to the councillor, it was just his way of having a laugh and a joke. The loud laughter caused Tommy to come out of his office to see what all the commotion was about.

"Are you in charge here?" asked Cllr Bumsgrove.

Tommy nodded in affirmation.

"My name is Cllr Bumsgrove of the town council and you had better excogitate a solution immediately for the situation or I warn you, I will be forced to throw my nomothetic weight around."

Big Barry burst into another fit of uncontrollable laughter.

"You want to watch that I don't throw *my* weight around!" he warned.

"He's right," said Tommy "You should watch out he doesn't eat you for his breakfast. Now, please leave us alone to get on with our business, goodbye Cllr Bumsgrove."

"You cannot just tell me to leave; I have the power to stay here until I have consummated my investigation of your unequivocal attempt at a business that I consider to be just utter floccinaucinihilipilification."

"Tha' flocking what?" asked Barry. "Has tha' eaten a dictionary for thee breakfast?"

Tommy turned to Barry.

"Ah, we have a sesquipedalian among us. The man likes to use big words to make out he's cleverer than we are, instead of portraying the ignoramus that he really is." Tommy took Bumsgrove by the arm and led him to the yard gate. "Now, if you wouldn't mind doing your consummating elsewhere, we can get back to our remunerative dexterous. Goodbye Cllr Bumsgrove."

The councillor left fuming; a feud had started. Had he entered the yard without such an attitude or had Tommy handled it another way, things might have turned out differently, but as far as Cllr Bumsgrove was concerned, a storm was coming and it was heading straight for Stumble Street.

*

Each day always seemed busy at the McCues' yard, although they worked for peanuts they made the most of the bad situation. It's funny to think that the hard work and the hours they put in didn't get to them; it didn't get them down, they always seemed happy. Perhaps it was because they had nothing with which to compare their job or perhaps they were intent on just being happy whether or not their life was hard or really hard. Perhaps they made the most of a bad hand dealt, with their laughter and the jokes to get them through. After all, to be miserable is one's own choice, is it not?

The burning gear was usually always on the go in the yard, cutting through large pieces of metal and making smaller pieces that were easier to handle. The gear looked like a hand-held gun with a long neck; it was connected to two rubber hoses, one going to a gas tank and the other to an oxygen tank. At the end of the gun was a nozzle where the two gases came together to form a very hot flame. Once the flame was applied to metal, it would soon start to glow red hot. There was a handle on the gun that could be pressed down to give the flame more oxygen, which would then start to melt the metal, and if this was done in a line you could cut through vehicle chassis, axles, steel sheets or anything else for that matter. You had to get the metal glowing hot before you added more oxygen, or the extra gas would just blow the flame out.

When the burning gear was in use, sparks would cover the area, but a skilled operator would angle the gun so the sparks and small pieces of dripping metal would divert, most of the time, away from the user. However, sometimes the metal would make a large cracking sound and spit back at you, so you had to be quick to turn your head away to guard your eyes and avoid being blinded. Goggles cost money, they were for wimps, and besides, you couldn't see what you were doing when wearing them. A hot piece of metal through your clothes was quite common; it was funny to see someone do a dance while quickly dropping their trousers or overalls shouting:

"Ooh y' bastard; ooh y' bastard! Aaaggghhh! Ooh y' bastard!"

Tommy and Barry took turns cutting up the shelter sheets or whatever else they had brought into the yard as scrap. They had always kept their heads down with the business, not really telling anyone what it was they did for a living, probably because nobody was bothered and didn't ask. Apart from obviously parking a car for sale in full view or servicing a car or two, everything else was of no interest to anyone but them. It worked well keeping out of the way of the authorities - out of sight, out of mind.

4
Kathy's Café

Just at the other side of the bus stop at Town End was Kathy's Café, a small white-fronted building with just one window at the front. It served the best breakfasts in town. Kathy owned the café, hence the name, and worked damned hard doing everything herself; cooking, serving and washing up. She lived upstairs above the café with her old grandma, whom she looked after.

Kathy was a pretty wee thing of about twenty-two, but her beauty was hard to see as she never had time for herself; her dark hair was always up and her blue apron was always on. She never seemed to stop running around serving, clearing, cooking and taking the money.

Kathy's Café was a regular place for Tommy and Big Barry. Usually after a few hours work, they'd break off for a late breakfast, more like a brunch really. The young men more often than not sat at the table next to the window.

The café had about six tables and was spotless inside. There was a counter along the back wall with doors to the kitchen. The stairs were behind it on the right wall as you walked in, also on the same wall was the door to the toilet, which was cosily placed under the stairs. You could hear the sound of the kitchen, the fat constantly frying in the pans. The tables were all covered with light green and white linen tablecloths and on top were little glass pots of salt and pepper with the café menu slotted in between. The woodchip walls were painted an off-white, which went well with the three pot ducks hanging on the left wall.

Kathy would come and take their order. Tommy and Barry

would always take the mickey and regularly play practical jokes on the poor girl; like the time Tommy saw her in town and asked if she would like a lift home in his new car that was parked just around the corner. Kathy seemed pleased not to have to walk home with all her shopping as Tommy opened the car door for her and sat her in the front. He then told her just to wait there for five minutes while he went to pick up something that he had forgotten to get from a shop. Kathy sat there waiting patiently, admiring the lovely interior of the car. About ten minutes later the real owner of the car returned, opened Kathy's door and asked what she was doing in his car!

Whilst she had a good sense of humour, Kathy was always far too overworked and run down to appreciate Tommy and Barry's juvenile mentality. I don't think they realised just how much pressure the young girl was under.

"Two Full Montys please, Kathy love, and two teas."

Kathy's Full Monty Breakfasts had everything; two sausages, two fried eggs, with their yolk tops white over, four rashers of crisp bacon, baked beans, tomatoes (the tinned ones), button mushrooms, fried black pudding, corned beef hash and a triangular piece of fried bread. Anything that was fried was done so in pork dripping. The Full Monty was accompanied with a large pile of bread and butter, which was served with a smile to the centre of the table.

"You're looking as gorgeous as ever, you know, those big blue eyes of yours are to die for," Tommy said.

"You talking to me?" asked Kathy.

"Well, I'm not taking to Barry!"

Barry looked up from tucking into his breakfast with quite a bit of it around his mouth and growled at Tommy.

"No, Kathy gorgeous, I was talking to you."

Kathy just gave Tommy a look that said; I know I'm not, so stop taking the piss, then off she went to wash up.

"Don't you think a beautiful woman, who doesn't think she's beautiful, looks even more beautiful?" Tommy asked Barry.

Barry, disturbed from his breakfast again, lifted his head.

"Why?" he asked.

"Because vanity is ugly, that's why."

Big Barry went back to his fodder rather than ask what vanity meant.

"Oh, never mind," said Tommy.

As Kathy came back out with the bread, Barry remarked:

"She's not got a bad pair of legs though…"

Kathy heard this and turned around as Barry continued.

"For a chicken!"

It was always water off a duck's back to her, and she made her way back into the kitchen.

While Barry finished his breakfast with the manners of an ape, he had a laugh with Tommy about their encounter that morning with Cllr Bumsgrove.

"The jumped up, two-faced, frosty, four-eyed, bald, buck-toothed little arse of a man."

The bell rang as the café door opened, it was Kathy's grandma.

"You're looking nice today, Mildred," said Tommy, "have you had your hair done?"

"Yes, I have, Tommy," she said, as she walked through the café on her way to the stairs. "I've been to that hairdresser next to your yard. He's very good," Mildred observed, "although his shop stinks of piss."

More often than not, while he finished his breakfast, Tommy

would browse through the daily papers he found on adjoining tables of the café. Now, as I've said, Tommy was a clever lad. Maybe if his circumstances had been a little different, he would have gone on to further education, even perhaps to a university and become a lawyer or possibly a doctor or something like that, but he had responsibilities that meant, for the foreseeable future at least, he had to carry on with his yard.

Tommy looked through the papers hoping he would find something that would give him a leg up the ladder. He was once told by his father that everyone is dealt a chance in life to make it big, and when that chance comes along, you have to grab it with both hands and work like mad not to let it go. Tommy longed to make something of himself and have a better life.

Although he didn't know it yet, Tommy's chance was about to be dealt, the question was would he notice it? If he did so, would he grab it? The hardest part of all would be if he did grab the chance, would he work like mad in the fight to hold on to it?

5

The Path of Fate

Tommy once bought a bus to scrap. He had sent Big Barry to collect it from Birmingham. It was a rough old thing and Barry had a terrible time bringing the bus back. There wasn't much diesel in the tank, so he took every opportunity to take the bus out of gear and freewheel it down a hill. By the time Barry had reached the yard everyone else had gone home for the night. He had just run out of diesel completely at the top of Stumble Street and the engine had stopped, but he was able to freewheel the bus into the yard, where luckily Tommy had left the gates open.

The following morning Tommy came into the yard at about eight o'clock, saw the bus and noticed Big Barry hadn't shut the gates the night before. He shook his head in despair at Barry leaving the gates open. If I've told him once, I've told him a thousand times, he thought as he headed up the stairs to his office.

"Tommy," a voice said.

Tommy looked around and saw no one.

"Tommy."

It seemed to be coming from the bus.

"Tommy, *help*!"

It was Big Barry stuck in the cab, which was quite small and Big

Barry filled it with his great mass. Tommy ran up to the bus.

"Oh, Tommy, thank goodness," Barry said in a weak voice.

"What the bloody hell are you doing?"

"I'm *stuck*! I've been here all night. Help me out will you?"

Tommy started to laugh.

"You big, fat daft bastard, why didn't you just drive to our house last night?"

"I've run out of diesel, that's why, now get me out of here. It's not funny, I've got cramp, I need a crap and I'm bastard freezing."

Tommy tried all ways get him out.

"How the hell did you get in there in the first place?"

Just then young Norman walked past on his way to school.

"Norman!" shouted Tommy, "I need a hand!"

Norman walked into the yard up to the bus and looked at Big Barry. Barry turned his head and looked at Norman's broad grin.

"Don't you say a flaming word," he warned.

Norman helped Tommy take the door off, but that didn't make any difference, then young Norman pondered the situation.

"Barry, they say if you don't eat, you can lose a stone or two a week. So, if you starve yourself for a while, you should have no problem getting out of there by say, the end of next month."

"*A aaggghhh*! Come here you little bastard!"

*

An hour or so later, Norman had had to go to school and Rosie had just arrived as Tommy was using the burning gear to cut the front of the cab off, covering Barry in sparks of hot metal. What a pair of pillocks, she thought to herself as she climbed the stairs to the office.

Finally, the bus gave birth to a healthy boy called Barry weighing in at about twenty-five stone. After a nice cup of tea, the same pair of pillocks set about cutting up the rest of the bus.

All the metal side panels were taken off and stacked up, the windows were taken out and the glass smashed up and stored in a small metal skip, ready to hopefully sell to the glassworks for recycling. The axles, engine and gearbox were also put aside to maybe scrap or sell on. The remaining metal would then be cut into pieces ready to sell, and the rest was just burned.

*

A few months later, Big Barry was just as big, so when Tommy purchased another bus, this time from Manchester, he had to go to fetch it. He thought he'd hitch a ride over the Pennines, so he stood early that morning on the corner of the Manchester Road with a piece of cardboard with 'Manchester' written on it, which he held up at the odd motorist in an attempt to catch a ride.

Car after car, lorry after lorry went by and time was getting on, but then an old 1949 Bedford pickup came around the corner. Tommy didn't like the look of it, but had a feeling it was going to stop. He tried to lower his cardboard sign, but it was too late and the pickup slowed and then pulled up. It was a mucky grey colour with a kind of a fence around its flatback. In the back were two dead cows and a dead horse, and by the smell of them they had been dead for a while. The driver got out looking a bit like a farmer; wellies, old tweed coat, flat cap and holey trousers. He was unshaven and dirty looking and had a piece of old string tied around his waist, holding his trousers up.

"Hello, you going to Manchester? I'm going to Manchester, do you want to go to Manchester?"

Bloody hell, Tommy thought. Of all the vehicles that could have stopped, I get this one. Tommy had been waiting for several hours and was desperate to get there. Desperate enough to endure a two-hour run in the smelly pickup. He didn't really have a choice.

"Yes please, if you don't mind," he answered.

As Tommy opened the passenger door an even greater stench hit him. Tommy took a deep breath before getting in with the hope he could hold it for two hours. In the cab there was one big seat across the middle where, in the centre, a billy goat sat, chewing at the seat. Down in the footwell was an old sheep dog gnawing at what looked like a sheep's head.

The driver introduced himself as they set off.

"My name's Charlie, yes, Charlie's my name. This is Billy the billy goat and down there is Roger-Sheep my sheep dog."

"All right, Charlie, I'm Tommy. I've got to ask you, Charlie, what are you doing with all the dead animals in the back?"

"Knackerman, that's what I am, I'm a knackerman. I collect dead animals and sell them to the dog food companies - sandwich?"

"No thanks," Tommy said as he watched Charlie get stuck into one. "What do you call your dog again?"

"Roger-Sheep," Charlie said with a mouthful.

"Don't you mean *Roger the Sheep Dog*?" asked Tommy.

"No it's Roger-Sheep," Charlie replied.

"That's a strange one, I haven't heard of a name like that before. Why did you call him Roger-Sheep?"

Charlie looked at Tommy seriously and said as he swallowed the last bit of his sandwich:

"Because that's what he does."

A few miles down the road the pickup stopped dead and Charlie got out. Tommy watched as he used his shovel to scrape up a dead fox from the road. He then carried it over and threw it into the back of his pickup.

"Waste not, want not!" he said to Tommy as he got back into the cab. "I got pulled up last week for drinking and driving you know, but I got off."

"How did you manage that?" asked Tommy.

"Well, they took me down the station and asked for a sample and I had to pee into a cup; do you know how hard that is when you've been drinking? Well, I put the cup on the counter and a police lady took it and came back with a cup of tea for the duty sergeant. I was arrested and they said they were going to take my licence from me. I told them that if I lost my licence, life wouldn't be worth living, I was going to go home, stick my head in the gas oven and end it all. Their consciences got the better of them, so they let me off with a warning!" He pointed to his head. "Up here for thinking." He pointed to his feet. "Down there for dancing!"

This guy wasn't as daft as he looked.

*

They made it to Manchester and Charlie dropped Tommy off right outside the place where he needed to be to collect the bus. He thanked Charlie and watched as he drove away; Tommy couldn't help but smile.

Tommy walked into the transport yard towards the main office where outside was the oldest, shabbiest looking double-decker bus he had ever seen. The tyres were bald, all the passenger seats had been dragged out and it was painted a horrible shade of greenie brown. Tommy took one look at it and thought, It's going to be one of those days. Just then it started to rain.

Tommy made his way to the office to quickly pay for the bus, so he could get straight off. As he walked into the office the staff there either turned away from Tommy or stepped back - he smelled like a billy goat. He went to the main desk and paid fifty pounds for the bus, which left him with nothing else in his pocket. He waited for the keys then ran through the rain to the bus.

As he climbed in, he noticed it had no front windscreen. He looked out of the window at the darker clouds gathering above the distant Pennines, knowing he was heading in that direction. He turned the key and there was nothing. Tommy could see the lads in the office laughing at him through the window, so he got out of the cab and ran back to the office.

"It won't start," he told them.

"Of course it won't," one of them said, "it's got no batteries!"

Tommy wasn't amused.

"Well, you had better get some and get this bus started."

By Tommy's look, the men in the office knew they should do what he said and get him some batteries, but they didn't have any to give. All they could do for Tommy was jump-start the bus. They brought another vehicle up to the side of the bus and ran the jump leads between, to where the batteries would have been. The bus started straightaway.

"Just make sure you don't stall it or you'll be walking home!" they said as they removed the leads and Tommy put the bus into gear.

As Tommy drove the bus out onto the road, he could feel the cold air race through the windscreen opening, and his hands soon felt very cold as the rain poured in. Black smoke belched out of the back through the exhaust and the noise of the engine knocking was almost deafening. He did stall it, but fortunately Tommy had just enough momentum to get him through the lights at Mottram where, just after the road went down a hill, he was able to bump start the engine. He drove through Tintwistle and up the road to the Pennines. The rain had turned to sleet and Tommy's hands had now turned to ice. The weather was getting worse, the wind was getting up; it looked like a storm was brewing.

Half an hour later Tommy was wet through and freezing. He had to pull over and, at the top of the Woodhead Pass, he saw a lay-by and pulled in. The whole area was filled with a cold murky fog. Tommy got out and left the bus ticking over, as he would not have been able to start it again, having no batteries. He ran around to take shelter in the back of the bus until the storm passed. He snuggled down into a corner on the bottom deck near the engine, in an effort to get warm, curled himself up into a ball and put his head on his knees.

The rain pounded the sides of the bus and the wind rocked it from side to side. He crouched there alone just thinking, and wondered if his dad would be looking down on him. Tommy was just about broke and, with the bills that were due to come in, the future wasn't looking bright. It was then he had a strange feeling while in that bus - as if his dad was with him. Tommy, ever the optimist, spoke.

"Dad, if that's you, will you shed a little light my way?"

The storm raged on for another hour or so then the rain stopped and the sun shone its face through the clouds. Tommy looked a little spooked. He got out of the bus, stared up at a rainbow that had just formed in the sky and smiled, then shook his head and made his way back to the cab where the bus was still ticking over.

As he did so he noticed what looked like a pile of copper pipes stacked up behind an old drystone wall. Tommy wasted no time in loading it all onto the bus. There was, he thought, about two grand's worth of copper. With this money he could pay all his debts off, expand his scrap business and much more. He couldn't believe his luck and carried on loading it all onto the bus. The copper filled the bottom deck and most of the top deck too.

He got back into the cab with a big smile on his face and then his conscience got the better of him. The copper didn't belong to him; it belonged to the owner of the field from where he had taken it. He sat there in the driver's seat deep in thought. What should I do? He felt that strange presence again, but this time it was different, like someone was watching him make his decision; was this temptation of copper put there as a test from up above?

Well, he thought long and hard before getting out and putting all the copper back. He felt it was the right thing to do, although he did it begrudgingly and the presence he had felt had gone. He drove off questioning himself as to what he had just done.

The old bus came down from the tops and Tommy put his foot on the brake pedal to slow down, but nothing happened - the brakes had gone. Now he was in trouble driving down from the Pennines with no brakes. He used the gears to slow the bus down and the idea had started to work, then *crack*! Something had gone in the engine - now he was in serious trouble.

The bus was up to about 60mph as it passed through Penistone town. The road had been fairly straight until now. Tommy was going through all the available routes in his head, routes that had the least bends, but they were all bad. There was a ninety-degree bend after the next village and it was looming ahead with Tommy unable to do anything about it. He overtook a couple of cars on the way down and then the bend came into sight. He took a deep breath as he approached it and started to turn the wheel in an effort to take the corner. The tyres screeched as the bus started to turn; it almost made it around before tearing off the road, down a steep bank and crashing into the woods, where it finally slid to a halt at the bottom.

In the woods, the bus was out of sight of the road and any passersby. It lay on its side in a bed of bluebells. The only sound was that of one of its wheels spinning, and as the wheel slowly stopped turning, the sound of the birds in the wood became more obvious.

Perhaps there was a debate going on in heaven, as to whether or not Tommy should live or die. Whether this was the case or not, Tommy didn't hang around to find out as he crawled out from where the windscreen should have been. He was okay, just a little battered and bruised, and very lucky. It was the bus that had died. There was no way it would make it back to be scrapped, so Tommy left it there and started the long walk home. He may have been lucky to walk away from that crash, but that bus had been the only collateral money he had, and he had just lost it.

As he walked home the heavens opened and the rain came down. Tommy reflected on his day from hell. How daft was he to leave all that copper and how unlucky that the brakes on the bus had gone? However, would a couple of tonnes of copper have given extra speed to the downhill ride? Yes, it would, he thought, if he had left the copper on the bus he would have come off the road and hit the wood with greater force. He really had had a lucky escape.

Darkness started to fall and Tommy still had a few miles left to go. He remembered the feeling that he had experienced in the lay-by - that his father was beside him. Maybe he was watching over him, and that thought made Tommy smile. It was in the early hours that Tommy made it home that night and he spent most of the next day in bed with a cold and a hot-water bottle.

The day he went to Manchester was probably one of the toughest days of Tommy's life, but it changed his outlook on everything - he didn't know why, but in some strange way he felt blessed. He had one life ahead of him and he intended to live it.

6

The Tender

It had been around three weeks since Tommy had seen an advert in a national paper regarding a tender for the sale of fifty old double-decker buses that London Transport was selling off. Not long after, Tommy had Rosie type a letter giving his tender bid for the buses. He had bid one hundred pounds per bus, a lot of money back then. The only problem Tommy faced was he couldn't afford one bus, never mind the five thousand pounds needed for the fifty.

Rosie was in her mid-fifties, she had worked part time for Tommy for a couple of years, although she had known him since he was a boy. Her husband, Ron, worked at the brickworks; a nice fellow, quiet and henpecked. Rosie always spoke her mind, especially if she didn't agree with something, and stood no nonsense. She was fiercely protective of Tommy and she also protected him from himself by keeping his feet on the ground. She wasn't scared to give Tommy her opinion if she thought he needed it. She wasn't very tall, so she always wore very high heels and kept her red hair up in a beehive to compensate. Rosie was good at her job, and she knew it.

With the bus tender Rosie had asked Tommy what the hell he thought he was doing. Tommy had a lot of respect for Rosie and it showed.

"Just type the letter," he had said.

To be honest, he never thought he would win the tender anyway, he just felt compelled to bid, a sort of destiny thing, but what about the money he would need if his bid was successful? Well, he thought, I'll cross that bridge if I come to it.

That day everything seemed to be happening, the little yard was really busy. Mrs Muff, a local lady who believed she was well-to-do, had brought her car into the yard. She was having problems with the mudflaps catching the kerbs when she reversed. Big Barry was just about to shorten them when the postman came into the yard and handed Rosie the post.

"More bills?" Tommy mumbled on his way past.

Mr McManus was due at any time to collect the latest pile of shelter sheets from Tommy. He had sold scrap metal to Mr McManus for a few years now, he always paid Tommy what he owed him. Tommy looked up to Mr McManus with great respect, high regard he thought he deserved, as he was a wealthy self-made man, although to look at him you wouldn't know it.

Mr McManus had come over from Ireland after the war. He travelled with the fairground as a ring fighter and later started work as a rag-and-bone man. He would, at one time, go from door to door at all hours and in all weathers with his horse and cart. His shoulders were massive and his hands were like shovels. His face was rugged with a couple of scars. He had the nose of a boxer and a cauliflower ear, but when you looked past the hard face and saw his eyes, you could see they were kind eyes. You would never mess with this no-nonsense hard man though, because you wouldn't really want to see his temper. He lived alone and although he had no family, Mr McManus never seemed the lonely type. He liked Tommy, although he would never show it. I think Tommy reminded him of himself years ago.

Young Norman was working in the yard again that day. He was

only fifteen, but only looked twelve. He lived on the same street as Tommy. Norman was still at school, however, if there was any chance of him getting away, he'd be off to McCue's yard to help out. Norman's mum and dad doted on him, especially his mother. This was because Norman was their only child. His older brother had died young from illness, and as you can imagine, it knocked Norman's family sideways. His parents did kind of encourage Norman to work for Tommy, in the hope that Tommy would one day give him a job when he left school, in order to keep their son away from the pits.

Rosie opened the post to find a letter from London Transport accepting Tommy's tender price. Payment had to be received by no later than three o'clock the following Friday afternoon, by hand to London Transport's head office located in a town hall within the City of London. The buses were then available from the transport depot located just outside the city, a short drive from their head office. Rosie looked at the amount of five thousand pounds, smiled and thought, This is going to be interesting!

Mr McManus arrived at the yard and together, with the help of Tommy and Norman, he loaded his lorry up with the old shelter sheets that Tommy had been collecting. Barry hadn't quite finished Mrs Muff's car, but as soon as he did, he would also help with the loading.

One of the soles on Norman's boots was coming off and Mr McManus noticed.

"Why don't you get some new boots, lad?" he enquired, putting his hand into his pocket.

"I can't afford any." Norman put it on a little, hoping the rich scrap man would buy him a new pair. "Yes, with the sole coming off the front it makes it hard to walk and it's very cold in winter."

Mr McManus pulled a large wad of cash out of his pocket, and Norman's face glowed. He took the rubber band from around the cash and gave it to Norman.

"Here," he said pointing to Norman's boot, "put this band around it!"

Norman's face was a picture as McManus put the cash back into his pocket; he couldn't work out if the Irishman was serious, taking the piss or just daft.

"Tommy, there's a letter for you!" Rosie shouted, with a big smirk on her face.

"Not now, Rosie!" Tommy shouted back, carrying a pile of heavy shelter sheets on his shoulder.

"I think you'll like to see this one!" she teased.

They had nearly finished loading and Big Barry was now helping as Tommy ran up the stairs to the office and read the letter. He then sat down in his chair not knowing whether to laugh or cry.

Just then Mr McManus walked into the office to pay for the shelter sheets.

"I reckon there is eighty pounds worth."

"No, there is a good ninety pounds worth," Tommy said.

"Eighty pounds and that's it; we can always unload the sheets back off my lorry!"

Tommy didn't seem his sharp self. Normally both he and Mr McManus would banter for ages before they agreed on the price, but Tommy came across as a little distant, his mind wasn't on the job.

Mrs Muff appeared.

"How much do I owe you, Tommy?"

"Oh, just see Rosie," he said. "Has Barry sorted you out?"

"Oh, yes," she replied as she walked over to Rosie's desk.

"What was it you had done?" Rosie asked,

"I've had my flaps trimmed," she said, and pulled out her cheque book.

As Mrs Muff bade farewell and left the office, Tommy took the eighty pounds from Mr McManus and handed it Rosie to count. Tommy knew after the wages and the bills he owed, he would only end up with about five pounds in his pocket. Well, at least his head was still above water.

Tommy then walked Mr McManus out, down the stairs and to his lorry. Mr McManus turned to him and offered some rare advice.

"There are no friends in business, Tommy, nobody will do you any favours. The sooner you learn this, the better."

The old Irishman then climbed into his lorry. Tommy nodded goodbye and was just about to push the door closed when he asked Mr McManus if he would like to purchase fifty double-decker bus bodies.

"How much?"

"Scrap value, one hundred pounds each, and I'm not taking anything less, before you start! Oh, and I get to keep the engines."

Mr McManus' ears pricked up as he got back out of his lorry.

"Where are they?"

"London," said Tommy.

"I'd want to see them first and I'd want them to be delivered to my yard in Sheffield."

"I can't deliver them for that price!"

"Well, you're going to have to if you want me to buy them!"

Tommy was back on form, it was this deal that was taking his mind off trying to get more money for the shelter sheets.

"To deliver them, I'd have to find fifty drivers and pay them to bring the buses back."

Mr McManus just shook his huge shoulders.

"Okay then," said Tommy, "but once you've scrapped them, I want the engines delivered to *my* yard and I'll need payment in advance."

The big Irishman thought for a minute.

"All right, when can I see them? I'm down near London myself next Friday, we should meet then and if they are okay I'll pay you on the spot."

The two men shook on the deal and exchanged details as to where they would meet the following Friday in London, then Mr McManus got back into his lorry and drove off down the cobbles of Stumble Street.

Tommy ran through in his mind the deal he had just done. For the cost of bringing fifty buses back from London, he would be the proud owner of fifty, 9.6 litre, five cylinder diesel engines, each potentially worth about two hundred pounds if shipped abroad. The only thing was, Tommy didn't know anyone abroad, but then, he thought, I'll cross that bridge when I come to it.

7

A Day Out

Friday soon came around. The bad news was the Austin car on the front of Tommy's yard hadn't sold, but the good news was they needed a car to get them to London. Tommy and Barry got into the car as Tommy said:

"I hope you've serviced this one properly."

"I have," said Barry as he squeezed himself behind the wheel, "and it runs and sounds like a Rolls Royce."

Rosie looked on with a disgruntled look, as if to say, what the bloody hell are they doing, going to London to pay for some old buses with no money? Tommy needed Big Barry to accompany him to check that the engines of the buses were okay before they paid for them.

As Tommy and Barry were just pulling out of the yard entrance, Cllr Bumsgrove was coming to see them and he was standing in the way of the Austin. Tommy wound the car window down just as the councillor spoke.

"Good morning, gentlemen. It would appear, due to your anomalistic antics, you have not paid your property rates for the last two years and I have here a final demand for immediate payment."

Tommy told the smirking councillor that all his buildings were not rateable because they were too small.

"So bog off!" he said, as he rolled up the paperwork and gave it back to the councillor.

Tommy and Barry set off laughing and waving goodbye to

Bumsgrove. The councillor was livid as he stood on the pavement and watched the little car drive off into the distance. He was going to close McCue's yard down, if it was the last thing he did.

*

The Austin did well on its way down to London, stopping only a couple of times to cool down, but it had taken Tommy longer than expected to get there. As they drove into the London Transport Depot, Tommy could see Mr McManus' car over by a very large industrial shed. Tommy and Barry parked up and entered the building. They were both taken aback by what they saw. The building was huge and in it were row upon row of bright red double-decker buses all parked perfectly parallel at an angle to the long side of the building. Tommy felt a fear of trepidation, as if he had bitten off more than he could chew.

As Mr McManus came into view, Tommy could see he had the same look, which didn't help Tommy's confidence. On top of that, Mr McManus had another look that told Tommy that he had been waiting there for too long.

"Sorry I'm late, Mr McManus, I misjudged the journey time."

Mr McManus was no fool and Tommy knew it, so Tommy was wise in situations like this. The best way forward was honesty, and Mr McManus appreciated it.

Big Barry had already palled the head mechanic of the depot and was at work starting up each bus. He could tell just by listening to an engine if it was all right or not. Tommy got talking to the depot manager; they seemed to get on quite well. Tommy joked with him to make sure he left enough diesel in the buses to get them to Yorkshire.

"What do you think, Mr McManus?" asked Tommy

"I think they're not worth five grand."

"Now, come on now," said Tommy. "We agreed on the five thousand."

Mr McManus knew he had agreed on the price, subject to seeing the buses, and the buses looked okay. However, he could see that Tommy was a little out of his depth, so there was no reason why he couldn't wind him up a little. Well, when I say a little, it went on for five or ten minutes. Finally, Mr McManus took a brown envelope filled with money out of his jacket and handed it to Tommy. Tommy looked at the money and his mouth dropped open.

Mr McManus then came down off his high horse and put his hand on Tommy's shoulder.

"There is a lot of money here, lad, don't blow it, and make bloody sure those buses get to my yard by next Friday."

The old, Irish hardened businessman would not normally trust anyone with that amount of money, but as I said, he liked Tommy, not forgetting the fact that Mr McManus was about to make a lot of money too. With that, he nodded his goodbyes, got back into his car and drove off.

The depot manager came over to Tommy and made arrangements for when he would be back to collect the buses, and it was agreed it would be the following Friday.

"Now, what about payment?" Tommy asked.

"Oh, you don't pay me, you need to take it to the town hall. It's about five miles away, but it will take you a good half hour, as the traffic through the city will be busy."

Tommy looked at his watch - twenty to three.

"Barry! Come on, we're going."

"I've just got a few more to check," Barry said.

"We haven't got the time," said Tommy. "If we don't get this money to the town hall by three o'clock, the deal's off and the buses will go back to tender."

They jumped into the car. This time Tommy was driving. He had got some rough directions to the town hall from the depot manager and off they went at speed. The depot manager had warned Tommy that the clerk in charge of the collection of the payment for the buses did things 'by the book'. If they didn't get the money to him by three o'clock prompt, the clerk's office would be closed and it would have all been a waste of time. The little car belted down the streets of London, Barry holding on to his seat and looking a little scared as the car screeched left and right. They went down a road filled with market stalls and Tommy caught one as he drove through.

"You just hit that stall!" shouted Barry.

"Shut up!" said Tommy.

Five to three, the town hall was in sight and Big Barry, still looking scared, let one rip in the car - the smell was awful. Tommy had to stop the car and get out. Barry couldn't stop laughing, but Tommy didn't think it was funny. Perhaps it would have been if he didn't have the responsibility of getting the money to the clerk by three o'clock.

"You dirty, smelly-arsed tosser!" Tommy told him.

After a minute or so they set off again. The town hall was a large stone building with steps leading to the main entrance. At the bottom of the steps was a flagged area with an ornate fountain in the middle. Tommy had no time to find a car parking space, so he drove past the fountain where the pigeons soon got out of the way. About three quarters of the way up the town hall steps he came to a stop and that's where he left Barry and the car as he rushed into the building.

*

Back at the yard, young Norman had wagged another day off school and had decided to take the crane out for a run. It was an old Coles crane with a single jib. It had no tracks, but ran on four, solid rubber wheels. He waited until Rosie had gone for a sandwich and then off he went for a pose around the town, with a little diversion past his school.

The crane was very noisy, which Norman liked, so he revved the engine even more as he went past the playground with a broad grin on his face. The only thing was, Norman had left the jib up and it was taking every phone line down as he passed. Young Norman was oblivious to all this, however, he did notice Rosie with her hands on her hips, standing just outside the sandwich shop at the bottom of School Street.

She shouted to Norman as he passed on his way back to the yard.

"You're pulling all the telephone lines down, *you pillock*!"

"What shall I do?" he shouted back.

"Keep going!"

*

Tommy entered the town hall and asked at reception where he could find the clerk responsible for receiving the payment. He was directed up to the third floor and into the office. There he found the clerk; a small man who was sitting behind a large desk. He was wearing a three-piece suit and he had dark rimmed glasses.

Tommy told the clerk he had come to make the payment of five thousand pounds for the London Transport buses. The 'jobsworth' looked at his pocket watch and told Tommy he was too late and that he had missed the deadline by a good two minutes.

"Now, if you will excuse me," he said, "I was just about to leave."

Tommy leaned over, grabbed the little man's lapels and lifted him over the desk.

"I have come a long way. I have brought some money, which you are going to count, and when you have finished you are going to give me the papers I need to release the buses. Now, do we understand each other?"

After a pause and a big gulp, the clerk's answer came.

"Would you like a cup of tea while I count the money?"

*

Outside a policeman had noticed the little Austin parked on the town hall steps. Big Barry gave a resigned sigh as he alighted from the car.

"Hello, hello, hello, who do we have here then, a pimp?"

"Pimp? Oh, I get it, town hall steps! Yes, very funny," said Barry, who looked a little worried and then farted once more. "Sorry about that."

"Is this your car, sir?" the policeman enquired, turning his nose away from the smell.

Barry didn't know what to say and the policeman was just about to get his notebook out when Tommy appeared, sporting a limp.

"Afternoon officer, sorry for parking here. It's just that I can't walk far and my good friend Barry here, helps me to get about."

We will never know if it was the terrible smell that Barry had produced or Tommy's silver tongue that made the policeman decide not to book them, but instead wave them on.

"Just don't park here again." The policeman then muttered under his breath, "bloody Northern oiks!"

Tommy reclined his seat a little and said:
"Okay, Barry, take me home."

8

Back at the Yard

Saturday morning and all was quiet. Tommy had been at the yard early and already emptied two cups of tea down the fireplace on the small landing next to his office, via his kidneys; well, they didn't have a toilet.

Tommy knew he needed fifty drivers for next week and it had dawned on him last night that the best place to do some recruiting was in the Shaft Club tonight, as Saturday was by far its busiest night. He would also telephone a few people he knew.

Rosie and young Norman came into the yard at about the same time.

"I tried to ring you last night, but I couldn't get through," Tommy told Rosie.

Rosie told him that was because all the phones were off in town.

"How's that?" he asked.

Rosie looked at Norman while answering Tommy.

"You know, I have no idea."

"I'm going to wash the Austin," Norman said quickly, and made a hasty retreat, much to Rosie's amusement.

Tommy decided to nip off for a haircut at the hairdressers-cum-barber shop next to his yard.

"I shan't be long," he shouted to Rosie as he left the yard.

He walked into the shop, a small converted front room of a house with just the one barber's chair facing a mirror on the adjacent wall. Gerald was a slight man who was a little effeminate.

"Hello, Tommy; just take a seat, I'll be with you in a moment," he said with a smile and a twinkle.

There were a couple of chairs by the window where Tommy sat down. The now legendary smell of urine in the shop was overpowering.

"Sorry for the smell, Tommy, but we just can't find its source. I've had to ask the council for help and they sent a funny little man around. He was as about as much use as a cushion is for a sore bottom."

Gerald lived with a lady called Lesley in the house next door to Tommy's yard. No one knew if she was his wife or just a relative; it's just that nobody seemed to ask. Lesley was a big lass, six foot tall and built like a brick shit house, her bleached blonde hair styled into what looked like a fireman's helmet. She usually kept herself away in the back of the shop while it was open. Apparently behind the five o'clock shadow and the hands like a bloke, she was quite a shy lady. However there was something strange about her though; but nobody could ever put their finger on it.

Gerald called Tommy over and sat him down in the barber's chair, where he flung a white sheet around his client.

"Are you having it off today?"

"Thy what?"

Tommy looked a little confused.

"Your hair, how much are you having off?"

"Oh, right. Err… short back and sides please and a bit off the top."

Gerald set about cutting Tommy's hair like a Picasso to a canvas, and when he had finished he dusted Tommy down with his little brush and then whisked off the sheet.

"Ta-dar!"

Tommy thanked and paid Gerald then got out of there as fast as he could, back to his yard.

*

Old Bert, a local chap, came into the yard office.

"Have y' had y' hair cut?" he enquired, looking at Tommy.

"Believe it or not, yes."

He told Tommy he had been talking to Big Barry and had heard he was looking for some drivers.

"Now, me and our Billy are available."

Old Bert was a retired miner. He was only in his late fifties, but had to retire because of his lungs. He had developed the early stages of emphysema. His knees were pretty knackered and his glasses were as thick as milk bottle bottoms.

"Okay," said Tommy, "but you're sure you both have a driving licence?"

"Oh yes, see you next week," Old Bert said as he left, passing Barry on the stairs.

"The only licence he's got is a fishing licence," said Barry. He scrutinised Tommy for a moment before saying, "Y've had your hair cut."

"Well, thanks for letting me know, Barry, sometimes I just don't know what I'd do without you. Are you going to the Shaft tonight, Rosie, because if you are, we need you to do some networking?"

"Yes I'm going to the club with my husband and no, I'm not networking, working, recruiting or anything else. I'm going to enjoy myself because Elvis is on."

"Who?" said Barry.

"What, the real one?" asked Tommy.

"No, you pillocks, it's someone impersonating him. His real name is Johnny Jackson, but he really does think he's Elvis; he's very good."

Tommy looked at Barry.

"Heaven help us."

It was time to break off and head for breakfast, but before they did, Tommy had heard that there was a little party going on at the town hall to celebrate Cllr Bumsgrove's promotion to 'senior' council officer.

Morning coffee was being served when Tommy walked in with a tray of sandwiches and handed them to the clerk at the reception.

"I'm delivering these sandwiches for Cllr Bumsgrove's party," said Tommy.

The clerk took them from him and told him he'd pass them on. He took them into the large room in the town hall where many councillors had gathered, and handed the sandwiches out. They went down a storm.

Tommy went back to the yard where Barry and Norman joined him and they all walked down to Kathy's Café together.

*

"Two Full Monty's, Kathy love, and a bacon sandwich for Norman," Tommy requested as he walked into the café.

While Kathy was in the kitchen, Tommy moved her till drawer and hid it under their table. When she came back through, Tommy said:

"He seemed a nice man who just came in to fix your till."

"What man?" Kathy asked as she noticed the till drawer was missing. "Which way did he go?"

"Up the road!" said Barry, and Kathy ran out through the doorway in hot pursuit.

It was about ten minutes later when Kathy came back almost in tears and she had a very angry look on her face.

"Where have you been?" asked Tommy.

"You know where, and none of you lot came to help me! That man's stolen my till drawer."

"Are you sure? As I said, he seemed a very nice man."

Kathy's suspicion made her look at the till once more, to find the drawer was in place. She opened it, all the money was still there and everyone on Tommy's table had a big grin on their face. Kathy turned, went back to her cooking and not long after brought the breakfasts out and served them to Tommy's table.

The breakfasts were burnt to a crisp.

"Sorry about the breakfasts, boys," she said, "it was silly of me to leave them cooking while I went up the road chasing a phantom crook. Now make sure you eat it all."

Nothing was said; the lads just picked up their knives and forks and started to eat like a bunch of naughty school kids who had just had a telling off.

Over burned breakfast, Tommy was putting his list of drivers together. He had only four on the list so far, and that included both himself and Barry, Old Bert and their kid.

"I'll drive one," said Norman.

"No, you won't, you're too bloody young," said Tommy.

Poor Norman looked like he was going to cry. He was desperate to go and drive a double-decker bus, and he had never been to London before. Tommy could see and understand Norman's frustration, but he didn't have a licence and that was that.

"I'll tell you what, Norman, see what your dad says about you taking a day off school and if it's okay with him, you can come along for the ride."

Young Norman's face lit up and off he went clutching his bacon butty, to ask his dad as soon as he could.

"Why don't you ask him when you get home? We're not setting off until next Friday!" Barry shouted after him. "That was nice of you sending the council those sandwiches," he said to Tommy.

"Yes," Tommy said, "I thought so; I made them with cat food you know."

The two fell about laughing. Kathy asked what Tommy's list was and as he told her, she started laughing.

"How much are you going to pay each of them to drive the buses back?" she asked.

"I'm not. Their payment is a trip to London and they get to drive a double-decker bus; it's a once in a lifetime opportunity," Tommy replied quite seriously, making Kathy laugh all the more.

She sat down at Tommy's table while Big Barry went for his constitutional.

"Okay, Tommy," she said, "suppose they accept that as payment, how are you going to get those in the club to talk to you, when most of them don't really like you?"

Tommy was taken aback at this. He'd never thought about it before, but Kathy was right - he wasn't one of them.

"Well, we'll just have to find someone we know who they do like to do most of the recruiting."

"And who's that then?" she asked.

Tommy just looked at her and smiled.

"Oh no," she said, "not in a million years."

9

A Night Out at The Shaft

Tommy had arranged to call for Kathy at her café and then meet Barry at the door of the club. He pulled on Kathy's knocker and after a moment or two, she came to the door. She looked a million dollars. Tommy was bowled over by her beauty, she looked a different person. He had to think of something to say quickly to compliment her and to stop him looking so damned love struck. After a long few seconds he managed to speak.

"Tha' brushes up well, lass."

They walked to the club and as they met Big Barry at the main entrance, an old guy, who was on the door, stopped Barry.

"Are you affiliated?" he enquired.

"Not any more," he replied. "Once I got some cream from the doctor it cleared up."

Tommy looked at Kathy, shaking his head in disbelief, and Kathy cringed somewhat at the thought. He told the old man that himself and Kathy were members and that they were signing Barry in. Tommy signed them all in using a number he had just made up. He thought he was clever, but soon had the wind knocked out of his sails when the old guy asked him for a cover charge of two bob each.

"What's that for?" asked Tommy.

The old guy on the door looked up and very proudly said:

"Elvis."

*

Tommy told Kathy and Barry as they entered the club, to stay out of the way of Councillor Pollock, because if he got wind of what they were up to he, being chairman of the club's committee, might throw them out.

In the foyer apart from the toilets were two doors, one on the right leading to the taproom and one on the left leading to the concert room. The bar was in the middle of these rooms, so the bar staff could serve both areas. In the taproom there were a lot of older men sitting enjoying a pint and a cigarette. At the bar was a team of lads, all downing pints, telling jokes and tall stories to each other. The decor in the room was a mixture of light green and nicotine, the tables and bar were dark stained and the carpets were worn.

In the corner of the room was a small round table and sitting there you would always find two local characters named Kipper and Spanner, more often than not, the worse for wear. Both in their late forties, they had been friends from school. Kipper was a miner, but he lived for his pigeons. He kept them on his allotment and had won many competitions racing them. At six foot, Spanner was about ten inches taller than Kipper and a bit bulkier around the waist. He also worked at the pit, but as a mechanic. They say he could fix just about anything that turned. The pair of them looked forward to their Saturday night out without their wives and if you ever met their other halves, you'd know why.

The concert room was much larger with a stage at the far end. There were lots of round tables that would seat about four. The tables were small, but big enough, however, for a few drinks and an ashtray. There were also a few stools at the bar and fixed seating all around the sides of the room.

Three barmaids, all with bubbly personalities, served the drinks.

Shirley was the main one, with a figure that was so shagedelic, she should have been in the movies. She was probably in her early thirties, but the hard work, the good times and the weather had made her look a few years older, although hard work kept her trim. All the men in the club drooled over her. She was quite tall and buxom, and wore her black hair up in a bun. Shirley knew she had great features and enjoyed showing them off too, with her low cut tops and her short skirts. She was a nice lass; a good-time girl and very obliging.

The other two barmaids were sisters, Sharon and Julie, both in their twenties. It was obvious Shirley was their role model, except when their dad was drinking in the club. If this was the case they were little angels.

Archie, the old club steward, made sure there was a constant flow of beer in the pumps and plenty of change in the tills. An old girl called Sweaty Betty collected and washed the glasses along with wiping the tables down. She always wore a sleeveless smock to work and constantly carried a tea towel. When she had her hands full of glasses, she would put the tea towel under her unshaven armpit and then she would use the same tea towel to polish the glasses. As Sweaty Betty walked past she gave Tommy a flirtatious smile.

"Bloody hell, she's rough, Barry. I bet you wouldn't like to wake up one morning and find that lying next to you," said Tommy, looking shocked.

Barry looked at Tommy.

"That's my auntie."

The folk in the club didn't like strangers or anything that went against routine. However, to know them was to love them, for they made the most of what they had and they certainly knew how to enjoy themselves. The club was full, but as yet, there was no sign of Elvis. Tommy, Barry and Kathy were busy recruiting. "How many have you got?" they kept asking each other.

Tommy and Barry were struggling; they were both getting the same two-word answer, with the second word ending in 'off'. Rosie had been watching them and couldn't help but smile as she sat with her husband near the stage, holding her half a bitter and black in a lady's glass. Kathy, on the other hand, was flying. All the men in the club seemed like putty in her hands. Rosie watched the chairman of the committee, Cllr Pollock, walking around, talking to folk as if he owned the place. She then saw him notice Tommy and got up to warn him, but it was too late.

"Tommy McCue! What are you doing in my club?" enquired Pollock, "and what are you doing going around to my customers with that sheet of paper?"

"Hello, Cllr Pollock! I was just looking for you, to ask for your kind permission to sell some raffle tickets for the church. They are raising money for a…"

"New roof!"

Kathy to the rescue!

"You can't just come in here and sell anything without asking," said Pollock.

"I've been looking for you to ask permission, councillor," said Tommy.

"In here it's 'chairman', and even if you had found me, I can't just decide like that, it's got to go before the committee.

After a good five minutes of creeping and praising the chairman, Tommy got a bollocking from Pollock, but seeing as it was for the church, he would allow it on this one occasion.

By now it was nine o'clock and there was still no sign of Elvis, but just then the main doors to the club were flung open, and in he walked; a dead ringer for Elvis, he had the hair, the clothes and the walk. He was met by the chairman's words:

"Where the bloody hell have you been?"

Elvis replied in an accent that resembled the American Deep South with a hint of Yorkshire.

"A well a, I'm a, so terribly sorry, sir. Ya see, well I was all ready for a night in. I was sitting in my favourite chair at home with my feet up, reading t'local paper, when I saw y' advert. I couldn't believe it, I thought, Well a bless a my soul, what's wrong with me? I thought, hot dam, I'm playing at T'Shaft. I tell ya, Lord Almighty, I could feel my temperature risin'. Anyhow, sir, I got here just as fast as I could."

Off he went to get ready. Silence filled the foyer. Pollock turned to look at everyone in disbelief, but during the commotion, Tommy and team had slipped away from Pollock and headed to the bar for a pint each for himself and Barry, and a ginger ale for Kathy.

"How many drivers have you got?" Kathy asked them with a smile.

"Ten," said Barry.

Tommy said he wasn't finished yet and needed more time.

"*How many*?" Barry and Kathy chorused.

"Four," Tommy said, trying to hide his embarrassment.

"Tommy, that's not you. Barry, Old Bert and their kid, is it? The same four on your list that you came in with, and did you know their kid is partially sighted?" said Kathy.

"Okay then, how many have you got, Kathy Smart Arse?"

"Oh, just twenty-eight," she replied.

Stanley was the club secretary and you usually found him sitting at the bar with a pint in one hand and a fag in the other. He was well into his sixties. Nobody knew if he was ever married, but there was a rumour he had a girlfriend had left him for the Pearly Gates many years ago and after her there would never be another. Stanley was thin and pale, with bloodshot eyes. They said that beer ran through his veins instead of blood and it was probably true, as his diet consisted of just beer and fags. He was a really nice man, who always seemed happy and content. Big Barry had asked Old Stanley if he would like to come with them all to London next week and drive a bus back. Old Stan jumped at the chance.

Tommy couldn't believe Barry had asked Stanley.

"The man's a walking corpse."

Elvis was introduced onto the stage by the club's tipsy compere, a little fellow in a flat cap called Charlie Blenkingsop.

"Ladies and gentleman and our 'impotent' guests, The Shaft Working Men's Club is proud to 'induce' a young man all the way from Memphis, California, a little town just outside err... New York. Please put your hands together and give a big warm Shaft welcome to *Mr Elvis Presley*!"

Elvis came on rocking. He was, as Rosie had said, very good; in fact he was bloody brilliant. He belted out song after song and strutted his stuff. It may have been just an old working men's club, but honestly, that night the atmosphere was like Vegas.

*

The next morning Tommy had asked Kathy if she wanted to take a picnic to the park to watch the local cricket team play. They arranged to meet in the park next to the old bandstand.

As Tommy got ready he seemed quite excited at the thought of spending the day with Kathy. He hadn't been to the park for years and it looked like it was going to be a lovely day. As he left his front door he was met by his cousin, Mable, who had her two little boys with her.

"Tommy, is your mother in?"

"No"

"Then *you'll* have to help me. I need you to look after Harry and Eddie while I go to work. Please, Tommy, I'm on my last warning."

Mable was a single mother who had a cleaning job at the hospital. Mrs McCue would always try to help her, as the poor lass had trouble helping herself.

"Mable, I've got to go somewhere. Isn't there anyone else who can babysit? Don't you know any prison officers or workhouse managers?"

"There's no one, Tommy. Please can you have them?"

Tommy couldn't believe his luck.

"Okay you two, but you'd better behave!"

"We will, Uncle Tommy," said Harry.

Little Eddie just smiled as Mable threw her arms around Tommy and gave him a big kiss on the cheek.

"I owe you one," she said as she ran off to work.

"Come on, we're going to the park for a picnic," Tommy said to them, and handed Harry one of his baskets to carry.

He returned to his house to find an old football that he gave to Eddie to carry.

*

In the park they met Kathy as planned by the bandstand.

"I didn't know you had kids," she said.

"I don't, they're my cousin's kids; this is Harry and this is Eddie."

ALLAN FINLAY

Kathy shook their hands.

"Pleased to meet you," she said. "How old are you, Harry?"

"Seven."

"And how old are you, Eddie?"

"Five and a quarter."

"Okay you two, clear off and play football. Stay where I can see you and away from the cricketers. I'll shout you when the food's ready," Tommy told them clearly, but looked a little apprehensive as he and Kathy made their way to the shade of a large sycamore tree on a bank overlooking the cricket field.

Tommy had brought some bits; a flask of tea, a couple of bottles of beer and a bottle of lemonade to make a shandy. Kathy came equipped with a wicker basket filled with sandwiches, pork pies, a quiche and a lovely home-made Victoria sponge. The cricket had already started and the home team was batting. Kathy spread the contents of her basket onto an old green picnic rug, the food looked delicious. Tommy wasted no time getting stuck in to a couple of the sandwiches and a pork pie.

The two kids ran around on the grass, stopping occasionally for something to eat and drink. The two boys came running over.

"Uncle Tommy, there are some older kids over there swearing. They have said the 'F' word, the 'B' word and the 'C' word, and you know what the 'C' word is don't you?" asked little Eddie.

Tommy looked at Kathy, not knowing which yes or no answer to give.

"No?" he chose.

"It's *crap*."

Tommy looked relieved.

"No it's not, Uncle Tommy," said older brother Harry, "it's *currant*." "Currant?"

69

Tommy looked confused.

"Yes, I heard one of the cricketers shout to a little boy who was on the score board roof, 'Get off that roof, you little currant!'.

Tommy smiled at their innocence. He told them that only thick people swear, because they have a lack of vocabulary, as they never learned the proper words to speak when they were at school.

"If you two start swearing it's because you haven't worked hard at school and, therefore, you're not as clever as you should be. So, if you want people to always think that you're clever, don't swear. Now bugger off and play football."

Kathy was quite impressed at the way Tommy spoke to the kids and the way they obviously looked up to him with respect. She asked him what his aspirations for life were. Tommy told her he just wanted to make something of his life, to get a few rungs up the ladder. Money didn't bother him.

Kathy didn't believe him about the money not bothering him, especially when it was all Tommy's business seemed to be about. He explained to her that money was the route to all evil and it was not going to be his route. Kathy didn't understand, so Tommy tried to explain.

"Have you ever seen a happy millionaire? No, you haven't, because there aren't any and that's because a millionaire builds his fortune on greed. He stands on his friends on his way up life's ladder just so he can become a rich man, and when he finally reaches his goal in life, he's lonely. His true friends have left him and they have been replaced by hangers-on; people pretending to be his friend, but in reality just want to be friends with his money. His greed will also have pushed him farther out of his comfort zone, making him stressed and insecure. I, on the other hand, am going to be a happy secure millionaire, enjoying the finer things in life, with true friends."

"Yeah, yeah, yeah," said Kathy.

Tommy asked Kathy the same question; what she wanted out of life.

"I don't know really," she replied.

There was a moment when their eyes suddenly met and they were about to kiss, when little Eddie came running up and shouted:

"Uncle Tommy, I need a poo!"

Now, Tommy was a bit squeamish when it came to things like that, especially when public conveniences were involved.

"Go and cross your legs," he said.

Kathy told him not to be so silly and to take Eddie to the toilet.

"Can *you* take him?" he asked her.

"He's *your* cousin," she answered.

"What if he catches something from the toilet seat? With those public toilets, you never know who's been sitting there before you. It happened to Big Barry you know."

"Uncle Tommy, it's coming out!"

While Kathy looked after Harry, Tommy picked up little Eddie and ran over to the gentlemen's toilets and into one of the cubicles. He whipped Eddie's trousers down and 'hovered' him over the pan, in an effort not to let him touch the toilet seat. He got there just in time and little Eddie did what he had to do. Tommy was straining, bent over with his back in an awkward position, and the smell added to his situation.

"Have you done yet?"

"*Nooo!*" and the little lad carried on.

Eddie's little face then showed a sign of relief, but soon

developed into a sign of concern.

"Uncle Tommy."

"What?"

"You didn't take my pants down!"

"*A aaggghhh!*"

*

Meanwhile, back in the park, Kathy was getting a little concerned, but then after about twenty minutes or so, Tommy and Eddie appeared.

"What kept you?" she enquired.

Tommy looked traumatised.

"Don't ask."

A group of lads had started to gather near the bandstand. At first glance they seemed a funny looking bunch carrying cases of all different sizes. Several of them looked quite geeky, some looked too fat and some looked too thin. It turned out to be a brass band from one of the collieries. Tommy recognised one of them.

"Look, there's Kipper!" he told Kathy.

Kipper was hung over and was sitting in the bandstand polishing the horn on his cornet. The group seemed to be waiting for someone.

At around three thirty the cricket finished, the home side had won and a large man had arrived to sort out the band. Kathy and Tommy watched as the band set up, finding it most amusing, as they were clumsy and very disorganised. The large man was obviously the band leader and conductor. He seemed rather stressed as he shouted at them all in his endeavour to get things organised. Even the members of the band were shouting at each other. A few people had gathered around the bandstand as the misfits started to tune up.

Harry and Eddie had come and sat down with Kathy and Tommy, who were giggling away as the conductor tapped his baton. Kipper looked like he didn't know what day it was and then the band started. It was beautiful! The giggling stopped as Kathy, Tommy and the boys became entranced with the music. 'Londonderry Air' was the first rendition. Who would have thought that this group of misfits could have produced such magic? The band continued to play for over an hour and gradually the small crowd had grown into a substantial one. When the band had finished the crowd gave them a much-deserved round of applause.

Tommy and the boys then walked Kathy home.

"I've really enjoyed today," she said.

Tommy agreed as they stood outside Kathy's café, then they said their goodbyes.

"Uncle Tommy; aren't you going to kiss her goodbye?" asked Harry.

"Shut up! I might have if you two little buggers weren't watching. Come on, it's time we got you home," and off they went.

10
The Preparation

Tommy had bought a very old single-decker bus that had a large cab in which Barry could fit. Big Barry had brought it back to the yard to convert it into a bus that would transport fifty men to London, would also act as a breakdown and, if necessary, tow a bus back. It would also carry some spare wheels and a couple of drums of diesel, along with a jack, tow ropes, chains and Barry's tools.

Tommy had asked Mr McManus if he could borrow his breakdown to take with them for use as a backup vehicle. Everything seemed set. The big worry was, however, would all the drivers turn up? They all had instructions to be at Kathy's Café at six o'clock on Friday morning.

*

On the Monday afternoon it was raining. A small slight figure in a raincoat had entered McCue's yard and walked up the steps to the office, where the man knocked on the door. Tommy answered to find it was Cllr Bumsgrove with some papers he had pulled out of his coat, which he handed to Tommy.

"What's this?" asked Tommy, leaving the councillor out in the rain.

"Due to the pollution of our town, I hereby give you written notice, which summons you to move off this site by the end on the month."

"Pollution?" said Tommy. "What pollution?"

Cllr Bumsgrove read from a list.

"The burning of tyres, the spillage of oil, the sonorousness of your crane and the fact that you don't have a toilet."

"You can't make me move just because of pollution," Tommy replied.

"I'm not," said Bumsgrove, "I'm making you move because you don't have planning permission for your business!" Bumsgrove could see by Tommy's face he had got him up against the ropes, so he carried on, "Also I've heard you are bringing fifty buses into the town, may I ask where you are going to park them all?"

Tommy was incensed.

"I am going to park them all around the town hall and make use of the town's free parking. Anyway, going back to the fact I don't have planning permission - I'll just put in for it."

Bumsgrove smiled.

"You could do that, but you will need to pay the planning fee, which would only be a waste of money for you, as I have it on good authority that the members of the planning committee will be told to refuse any application you make. You will find the usage of our chief whip perfectly legal. Good day, Mr McCue."

"Did you have a nice party the other morning? I heard the sandwiches were very good," Tommy shouted to him as he left.

The councillor turned, looking puzzled.

"Yes, they were very good."

"I made them," said Tommy, "with cat food - *meeoow*!"

Bumsgrove felt sick as he looked angrily at the conceited Tommy then off he went turning right out of the yard and up Stumble Street. What a shambles!

Tommy read through the papers. The planning fee was a thousand pounds. Now he knew he had been stitched up.

Kipper came into the yard and asked if he and his mate, Spanner, could come and drive a couple of buses back.

"We asked you the other night, Kipper, we've already got you and Spanner on the list."

"Have ya'; I don't remember," said Kipper, looking confused.

Tommy told him where to meet and hoped he'd remember.

*

Tommy sat on the wall of the yard in the rain trying to think with the weight of the world on his shoulders, going through everything in his head about bringing the buses back and his problem with the planning permission, when Mable walked passed with her kids and shouted to Tommy.

"Where are our Eddie's pants?"

Tommy looked up from his deep thought.

"What?"

"Eddie's pants; he had them on when he went to the park with you the other day and now they're missing," she said. "Have you got them?"

"Have I bloody hell!"

Tommy didn't know what she was talking about until he saw an embarrassed look on little Eddie's face that said, 'Don't tell m' mum I pooed m' pants'.

"I don't know, Mable. Why the big issue?" asked Tommy, who at that moment had more important things on his mind.

"Those pants," she said, "were the only pair he'd got and I can't afford to get him any more until I get paid at the end of the month."

Tommy reached into his pocket and pulled out his last pound.

"Here, go and get him a new pair and get Harry something with the change." He then whispered into little Eddie's ear, "You owe me one, poopy-pants."

*

That night Tommy's mother had noticed that he seemed down, which she thought peculiar as everything seemed to be going well for her son, what with the forthcoming London trip and all. Tommy told her he was just a little tired. He would never let any of his problems through to his mother, always telling her everything was fine.

Mrs McCue always fed her son well, and all home-made stuff too. Any chance Big Barry could get in for a meal, he would. He especially liked her home-made soup she called 'sticky rib', as when you drank the soup it stuck to your ribs on the way down to your belly - it worked best on a cold day. Often she would fill a flask for Tommy to give to his men. The sticky rib soup was a thick soup made with lentils, turnip, carrots, onion and a pinch of garlic. It was brought together with a home-made ham stock and finished with plenty of salt and pepper.

Anyway, home-made food or not, the reality was Tommy was down and he didn't know what to do. Whatever the planning fee was, it was pointless, as any application he made would be refused. Even if he went ahead with an application, paid the thousand pounds that he didn't have and got permission, it would only be false economy, as he could buy another larger yard for less with the relevant planning permission, on the outskirts of the town.

The timing was also an issue; where would he store fifty engines in the meantime? The end of the month was when he had to be off the yard and that date would soon come around. The worry of this and everything else was getting to him, including the fact that London Transport had Mr McManus' five grand. The one thing he couldn't do was let Mr McManus down. Needless to say, Tommy didn't get much sleep that night.

*

A couple of days later, Tommy made the trip to Mr McManus' yard to pick up the breakdown he was going to borrow. Mr McManus told him, in no uncertain terms, that the breakdown should be returned full of diesel and without a mark on her. The breakdown was huge; it had been converted from an old AEC Mammoth Major eight-wheeler flatback. It had been painted red with the name 'McManus' on the doors. There was an orange flashing light on the cab roof and just above the windscreen was the breakdown's name, 'Big Bertha'.

Mr McManus' work ethic was, never put off until tomorrow a job you can do today. The breakdown was always fuelled up and always immaculate, as was his yard. He took pride in everything being in order, as he knew it all reflected on him and his firm. His men had worked for him for years; he looked after them and respected them. They, in turn, worked hard and had mutual respect for their old boss.

Mr McManus could see Tommy was troubled.

"Is it the fact you owe me five grand's worth of bus bodies? Have you bit off more than you can chew, laddie?" he teased.

Tommy shook his head and told Mr McManus the problem he had with the council, the fact that he didn't have planning permission on his yard and the thousand pound planning fee they required. Old McManus knew he could lend Tommy the money, but letting Tommy sort it out himself would do the lad more good. The experience would make Tommy a little wiser and a little harder, just what he needed, Mr McManus thought, if Tommy was to make it as a businessman in these hard times. He told Tommy that if making money was easy then everybody would be doing it.

"If you want to go it alone, you are going to have to accept the fact that it is inevitable a lot of people will become jealous of you, and there will be certain ones, usually the nobodies in life, who will try all they can to get in your way and pull you down. People like that get incensed because they have not been able to do or achieve what it is you're doing. Now, get yourself some legal advice from a good solicitor. I can recommend one to you if you like, and in the meantime, mess this bloody councillor around as much as you can, you might even enjoy it!"

Tommy smiled and thanked the wise old Irishman. He had given him a little glimmer of hope and that's all that Tommy needed. He felt a lot better, his chin had been lifted and with that Tommy climbed into Big Bertha and drove out of Mr McManus' yard.

*

Friday was soon coming around; 'Tommy's trip' was the talk of the town. Parked on Stumble Street outside McCue's yard were Big Bertha and the bus breakdown that Barry had converted. This would be the vehicle Barry would be driving, so after seeing Tommy had a name for his vehicle, Barry christened his, 'Brenda'.

It was decided not to leave the two breakdowns at the yard that night, just in case they were tampered with. Barry would take Brenda home and Tommy would spend the night with Big Bertha. It has to be said, both Brenda and Big Bertha looked two impressive vehicles parked outside McCue's yard that day. The sight of them had helped recruit the last few remaining drivers needed to make up the fifty.

All was about set. Tommy asked Rosie if she would be at Mr. McManus' yard the following evening to count the buses in and take a record of the engine numbers and engine types.

"And don't forget to look after my yard while the troops are away!"

With that they locked up, and Rosie and Norman set off on their separate ways home.

"Don't you be late in the morning, Norman!" shouted Tommy. "Six o'clock at Kathy's Café!"

Tommy and Barry climbed into their chosen vehicles, fired them up and off they drove.

11
The Expedition

Norman opened his eyes and not long after, realised he had overslept.

"Oh, my goodness!" he shouted as he rushed to get dressed, and then out of the door he flew.

He sprinted all the way down to Kathy's Café. When he got there, everyone else was getting onto Brenda, Barry's breakdown bus, which had Big Bertha hitched to the back. Tommy noticed Kathy handing out bacon sandwiches. What he hadn't realised was Kathy had promised them all breakfast while she was recruiting in the club.

"You didn't have to go to all this trouble," Tommy told her.

She just smiled at him.

"I know," she said. "Have a good trip, I'll see you when you get back."

They looked like a right set of Raggy Arsed Lads as they all boarded the bus. Big Barry said he would drive the first leg. Tommy was counting everyone on.

"Who asked Elvis?"

Barry gave him a big grin and shrugged his shoulders.

"All right, Stanley!"

Stanley went on with a can of beer instead of a bacon sandwich. Tommy took it from him, so he went on with just a fag. Old Bert brought their Billy, whose glasses were double the thickness of Bert's.

"All right, Bill!" Tommy said, but there was no answer.

Bert told Tommy that he thought their Billy needed his ears syringing.

"I've told him several times, Tommy, but he never listens."

Everybody was on and ready to go. All the seats were taken, along with a couple sitting on the diesel drums and the rest standing or finding their own place on the floor. Three or four of them had found a more comfortable place in the cab of Big Bertha, elevated securely on the towing rig of Brenda. Norman had found a good spot on top of the pile of old tow ropes. There were two large boxes at the front of the bus, Tommy asked what they were.

"They're m' pigeons, I'm taking them to London to let them go; they're homing," was Kipper's reply.

"They're *humming*," said Spanner.

Tommy told Kipper to take them out and put them on the back of the breakdown, so as to give the lads a little more room on the bus. They all waited patiently for the bus to start. After a couple of minutes Tommy got up to see Big Barry wasn't in the driver's seat.

"Where the hell is Barry?"

"He's gone for a crap!" said a voice from the back.

A few minutes later, Barry came out of the café to a big cheer from the lads. As he passed Kathy on the pavement he said:

"I'm really sorry, Kath, your flush has broken and I've lost the end off your bog brush."

"*Barry*!" she shouted.

Barry gave an apologetic shrug of his shoulders as he headed for the driver's seat and climbed in the cab. He turned the key and Brenda roared into life. He turned to Tommy for the okay and Tommy nodded to go. Cheers filled the bus. Kathy waved them off and away they went.

In the back all the Raggy Arsed Lads were crammed in and Tommy was listening to their conversations, becoming a little worried when he realised most of the talk was about how to drive. Questions were being asked such as, 'so, which pedal is the clutch?' However, Tommy did feel a little relieved as he had crossed the first major hurdle; all the drivers were there and they were finally on their way.

It wasn't long before the lads got Elvis up, he didn't take too much persuading. Old Stanley then told a funny story about the time a girl he had fancied for years came up to him for the first time while he was standing at a bar. That day Stanley couldn't find his belt, so had to go out without it. As the girl approached him, his trousers fell down to his ankles - she didn't notice. Stanley knew if he bent down to pick them up she would not only notice that his trousers had fallen down, but also the fact that he didn't just forget his belt that day; he had forgotten his pants too! He stood there for an hour chatting her up.

"Now, to do that with your trousers down and your old man hanging out takes concentration you know!"

*

Once Barry reached Peterborough it was agreed he would pull in and swap with Tommy to share the driving. Barry pulled in at a roadside café bearing the name 'Greasy Vera's'. It looked dingy and horrible, but that didn't stop the lads nipping in for a quick cup of tea as they stretched their legs. Tommy didn't let them stay long, he soon got them all back on the bus.

One of the lads, Hard Man Ray, had noticed on the way down that young Norman's place on the ropes looked more comfortable than his own position on the bus, which was standing up, looking hard, so he had taken it, leaving Norman to stand. Hard Man Ray was not well liked around the town. He was a known local troublemaker, who had somehow bullied his way into being part of the adventure. He was about thirty, stocky and vain. His hair was combed back into a ponytail. His shirt was unbuttoned halfway down and his sleeves were always rolled up so you could see his tattoos.

Otherwise, the atmosphere on the bus was great; it mirrored that of a good lads' night out. Stanley was sitting happy and content, as this was the best thing he had done in years and I think that went for a few of the others too. A lot of them had come straight from their shift and it wasn't long before many of them were catching up on their sleep.

*

A couple of hours after Tommy had taken over the wheel they came into the City of London. As they drove, the sight of a bus pulling a breakdown got a few double takes from the locals.

Anyone who had been asleep had now been awakened. As it turned out, most of them hadn't been to London before. They were all in awe of the fabulous buildings and the well-dressed people they saw within the great city.

"Buckingham Palace!" someone shouted.

They all scrambled for a look as they drove past. Just about three or four miles out of the city, Tommy pulled into the London Transport Depot. He parked adjacent to the large shed that housed the buses.

The workers of the transport depot stopped and stared at the sight of Big Bertha on the back of Brenda. Their mouths dropped open when they saw the Raggy Arsed Lads getting out, all crippled with cramp from the journey. Old Bert's voice could be heard above the rest.

"Ooh, m' bastard legs!"

The depot manager came out to meet Tommy, and they shook hands. The manager told him that he had, as promised, made sure all the buses had enough diesel in the tanks to get them back to Yorkshire. He also said because the new buses that London Transport had just had delivered were equipped with radios, there had been no need to take the old radios out of the buses Tommy had purchased.

"So, you can listen to music all the way home," he said. "Also there are a good few of your buses that still have their shortwave radios installed."

This was great news, as Brenda and Big Bertha had shortwave radios too and it would make it a lot easier keeping in contact with everyone on the way back.

Barry in the meantime had uncoupled Big Bertha with the help of Norman. He also got the diesel out and gave his Brenda a good filling up. Most of the other lads were having a smoke on a nearby grass bank, taking advantage of the fresh air and the warm sun coming out. It looked like it was turning into a nice day. Kipper unloaded his pigeons and lifted the lids to the boxes, but the pigeons just looked at him.

"Go on y'!" he shouted as he shook the boxes, then about fifty pigeons took off and headed for Tommy and the depot manager, crapping on Old Bert on the way.

"*Duck*!" the depot manager shouted as the pigeons flew low.

"No, I think they're pigeons," Tommy replied.

The birds then doubled back towards the lads on the grass bank.

"Incoming!" someone shouted; then off they flew out of sight.

"Come on!" shouted Kipper. "We've got to beat them home!"

The rest of them had a wander around while Tommy and Barry got things sorted. One of the lads, who was known as 'Digger', asked Old Bert to go over the gears with him once again.

Tommy gave the depot manager a drink, just a few bob, just to thank him for his trouble. The manager had done Tommy a big favour fuelling the buses up, and he hoped that if he sold the engines, he would be back one day for some more buses.

Tommy got all the men together and gave them instructions to stay in convoy, so none of them got lost. Big Bertha would lead and Brenda would be tail scout.

"Those of you who have shortwave radios, set them to channel fifteen and apparently 252 LW is a good frequency for music. We will stop for a break again at the café at Peterborough. Norman, you're with me." Tommy also gave everyone the address for Mr McManus' yard, just in case anyone got lost. "Okay men! Go and get yourself a bus… and take it steady!"

Off they all ran to try and get a bus with a shortwave radio then Big Barry checked everyone was okay.

"Tommy, we're two drivers short!"

"Oh, bollocks!"

Tommy hadn't accounted for himself and Barry driving the breakdowns.

"I'll drive one!" said Norman.

"No you bloody won't!" said Tommy. "Bollocks, bollocks and bollocks!"

He went into deep thought.

"Why don't you just put the two spare buses on the breakdowns?" Norman suggested, realising he wouldn't be driving.

Tommy and Barry looked at each other as if to say, 'that was too obvious a solution to think of'.

"Okay, but let's hope we don't have any of the other buses breakdown en route," said Barry.

"Well, if they do, just swap them for one of the good ones that are being towed on your breakdowns," said Norman.

Tommy and Barry looked at each other again. With that, Big Barry got straight on with hooking up the two spare buses.

Bert shouted to Tommy to come quickly.

"What's the matter?" asked Tommy, running over.

"It's old Stanley," said Bert, "he's *dead*."

Tommy looked over at the bus Stanley was about to drive and there he was, sitting in the cab with a smile on his face and a fag in his mouth.

"Have you checked his pulse?"

"Yes, and he's dead."

"Oh, bollocks." Tommy didn't know what to do. A few had gathered around. "We need to call the police."

"No, we need to take Stanley back home with us; we can't just leave him here all alone. During the war we never left anyone, we need to take him home," said Old Bert.

There was an agreed consensus at Bert's words. Tommy asked a couple of them to take Stanley and sit him on a seat in the bus. It seemed only right that they took him home. Now they were a driver short. Tommy looked at Norman, who was sporting a big smile.

"Okay, Norman, you're on, but take that grin off your face. It's not right to be smiling at someone else's misfortune, and another thing, don't tell your mother you've been driving!"

Norman's smile soon disappeared.

"I'm not driving that one; it's got a dead body in it."

"Shut up, Norman, take it or leave it," Tommy said.

Norman was so desperate to drive, he reluctantly agreed then jumped into Stanley's bus and started it up.

One by one the buses started. Smoke filled the large shed and the noise of the engines filled the team with excitement. Hard Man Ray came up to Norman's bus and asked if his bus had a shortwave radio. When he found it had, he told Norman to get out and swap buses. Norman didn't argue, in fact he was glad to get away from the bus that had a dead body in it. Ray on the other hand knew nothing about old Stanley; he was just pleased he had now got himself a shortwave.

All the radios were tuned into the frequency Tommy had given them, turned up to the sound of The Four Season's, 'Sherry Baby'. Big Bertha's eight-cylinder started and revved up high. Tommy pulled on the horn, put her into gear and the wheels started to roll. Like a big red train they meandered slowly out of the transport depot and onto the main road towards the big city.

Tommy felt a great rush of adrenalin as he led the pack in Big Bertha. Several buses back was Hard Man Ray, struggling with the gears. Old Stanley looked happy in the back of Ray's bus. To be honest, Stanley didn't look much different dead as he had when he was alive. A couple of buses behind Ray was Bert, followed by their kid, Billy, who seemed to be straining to see the road through his thick glasses. Elvis was somewhere behind them. You could hear the loud grating of Digger's gearbox as he got used to the gears. Norman was near the back of the pack with his radio on full blast, but the first chance he got he would make his move towards the front. A few more buses then it was Big Barry bringing up the rear, towing a double-decker. With a rolled up cigarette in his mouth and his large elbow sticking out of the open window of Brenda, Big Barry was in his element.

Tommy didn't rightly know if bringing all the buses back in this way was legal, after all, he only had insurance for the breakdowns. Either way he thought the best bet was to keep away from the police. No sooner had he thought 'police', than Tommy pulled up to a red light, where a policeman was sitting, parked on his motorbike. Tommy looked at the policeman and nodded good day, the policeman nodded back. The lights went green and Tommy drove on.

Tommy was straight on to the shortwave radio to warn the others. The lights turned red again. This time it was Old 'Bottle Bottomed' Bert who came to a halt at the lights. He looked at the policeman and nodded. The policeman reciprocated. Bert was just about to nod back again when their Billy ran straight into the back of him, knocking Bert through the red light. Bert got on the radio.

"Tommy, our kid's just hit me up the arse at the lights."

"What have you done?" asked Tommy.

"I kept going!" said Bert.

"What did the policeman do?"

"He put his hands over his head and made a strange expression with his face."

The policeman looked back in disbelief as this time he did a double take at the double-decker at the traffic lights. Elvis lifted his hand, smiled and waved; the policeman in shock lifted his hand and waved back.

The buses rolled into the capital, past the palace, up The Mall and around Trafalgar Square. Spanner got on the shortwave.

"Kipper, I think them's your pigeons 'aving a bath in that fountain!"

Everyone looked.

"I think Spanner's right," someone said.

Kipper seemed worried as he picked up the microphone to the shortwave.

"They'll be okay; they're homing."

"They're *roaming*!" said a voice.

At the end of The Strand was a bus stop, where a bunch of American tourists were waiting for a sightseeing trip. As the buses drove past, the Americans couldn't believe that there were so many buses in London. The traffic on The Strand had got quite congested and sure enough the buses started to back up and come to a standstill. Young Norman's bus stopped right at the bus stop where the Americans were and they all got on. Norman noticed nothing from his drivers cab, as his head was in the music and his mind was on overtaking. The convoy made its way through Holborn and on its way to Islington where it would meet the Great North Road.

There was a bus stop in Islington where several people had been waiting for some time.

"Look at that, you wait ages for a bus; then fifty turn up at once," said one chap at the bus stop as he saw the buses coming towards them.

The man put his hand out, but none of them stopped. After seeing Norman drive past with a big grin on his face, the man said to the old lady standing next to him:

"You know you're getting older when bus drivers start looking younger."

They came to a roundabout and all the buses went around it apart from Old Bert and their Billy, who went over it. It was then onto the Great North Road.

*

Meanwhile, back at the town hall on the third floor, in his little office that had a large window overlooking the council dustbins, Cllr Bumsgrove was going through several piles of files on his desk, looking for evidence to back up his claim that Tommy didn't have planning permission. The councillor's smug look turned increasingly into a big grin - this time he knew he could close Tommy down and it would be for good.

*

Norman made his move to overtake; he got past four or five over the next few miles. As Norman passed Elvis to the sound of Martha Reeves and the Vandellas, he waved an 'I'm beating you' wave to him. Elvis then noticed that Norman's bus had passengers on it, and he laughed uncontrollably.

"Tommy, my boy!"

"Come back, Elvis. Over."

No reply.

"*Elvis*!"

Still no response.

"Elvis, what is it?"

Elvis clicked the mike to let Tommy know what the problem was. All Tommy heard was Elvis trying to stop laughing so he could tell him what it was he needed to tell him.

"It's Norman…" More laughter. "Oh, Lord… Ah, ha, ha, ah… Norman's got *passengers* on his bus!"

Elvis was in pain trying to stop laughing and it was contagious too; everyone with a shortwave was laughing. Big Barry at the back could hardly breathe for laughing.

"Y' what? Over," said Tommy.

"Er… there's passengers on Norman's bus, and one of them is

wearing a ten-gallon hat!"

Elvis couldn't talk any more.

Tommy got on the radio to Norman, but there was no answer. Hard Man Ray came on the shortwave and told Tommy that he had swapped buses with Norman and he didn't have a shortwave. Tommy was mad at Ray for bullying Norman into not having a radio. He thought about what to do; he knew stopping fifty buses would take up too much time, so he decided they would drop Norman's passengers off at Peterborough. Finally he saw the funny side - it could only happen to Norman.

Now, back then the Great North Road didn't have the town bypasses it has today, so the convoy of buses had to drive through quite a few towns and villages. One particular town was Biggleswade, and that afternoon they were having a country fair. Banners and flags lined the main street, there were stalls selling all sorts, and livestock was on show in pens. The whole town was out; it really was a beautiful day. The local mayor and mayoress were decked out in all their regalia. Ducks, geese, cows, sheep, chickens and pigeons were the sound of the country. The stalls were busy, selling everything from fresh meat to eggs, and country clothing to toys and pets. All the local shops, the butcher, the baker and the greengrocer, were open and all were very busy. The butcher, a large man with a big red face, was rubbing his hands together at all the money he was taking. There were some old vintage tractors on show; you could hear one of them as it started up.

Lots of people heard the tractor's engine, but somehow it seemed to get louder and louder, then the noise appeared to be coming from somewhere else. The locals' eyes followed their ears to see Big Bertha, followed by fifty double-decker buses coming over the hill towards the town.

It was like a parade entering the town. The bus being towed by Big Bertha was elevated at the front, hooked to the back of the breakdown with its front wheels off the ground. This gave the front of the bus extra height to reach a string of flags that was attached to the butcher's shop. The bus caught them, which pulled the front of the butcher's shop out.

Tommy immediately realised what he had done and two choices came straight into his head. The first was, Should I stop and pay for the damage? The second was, Should I put my foot down and get as far away from this town as I can? The second option seemed more appealing, so it was the one Tommy went for. He got on the shortwave radio.

"We have had a little mishap, so we all need to get out of this little town as soon as possible."

All the ones with a shortwave put their foot down. Those who didn't have a shortwave, like Norman, thought the race had started, so they put their foot down too.

Two of the drivers, Daft Dave and Grizzly, were a right pair of silly sods. Grizzly couldn't resist clipping the egg stall and over it went, sending eggs flying everywhere. What Grizzly could do, Daft Dave could do better. He saw a nice big puddle in front of the mayor and mayoress, and diverted to take advantage of the opportunity. The two dignitaries, along with all the members of their party, were covered in a wave of water as Daft Dave's double-decker splashed through. Old Bert slowed down to see the commotion and their Billy ran into the back of him again. Thank goodness Daft Dave was near the back of the convoy, which meant only a few buses followed him through the craft tent before rejoining the rest of the group. Barry was crying with laughter.

"This is the best goddamned sightseeing trip I've ever been on. It's better than those rides at Disney!" exclaimed one of the Americans on Norman's bus.

*

At last Tommy found the road out of the town and guided Big Bertha back towards the Great North Road. He checked with Barry at the back to see if all were present and correct.

"We're all present," Barry came back, "but I don't know about correct!"

Norman had made it halfway up the pack by the time Tommy pulled into the roadside café on the eastern side of Peterborough. All the buses parked in the lorry park around the café. Bert asked Barry to sort out a tyre that had gone flat on his bus. Norman went to help and he and Barry set about changing it.

"That was funny with you picking up those passengers, Norman," Barry said, laughing.

"What passengers?" Norman asked.

The Americans entered Greasy Vera's Café, they asked who was in charge and Tommy was pointed out. Tommy saw them coming towards him, there was to be no escape. What could he do? It was just one of those things; he prepared himself for a bollocking.

"Hey, boy!" said the man in the ten-gallon hat. "This is a fantastic tour, let me tell ya. I can't believe you don't have more customers, is this the quiet season?"

Just then Elvis brushed past.

"Pardon me, sir... ma'am."

"We are not very busy at the moment; it's a new business. Now, would you like to get off here or in Sheffield?" asked Tommy.

They wanted to know if they could go back to London, but Tommy explained that it was a twin city tour where you got the train back the next day.

"Well then, I think we'll go to Sheffield, my boy!"

"Okay, would you like to pay now?"

Tommy got fifty pounds out of the deal!

Grizzly's bus had been blowing out black smoke over the last few miles up to Peterborough, so Tommy had decided to swap it for the bus on the back of Brenda.

Most of the lads had brought a snap box with them and a lot queued up for a cup of tea behind Tommy, which he said he would buy them. Once Tommy had what he needed, he headed for the pay desk.

"My dad's paying for this, he's at the back of the queue," he said to the girl at the till as he pointed to Old Bert.

The young girl rung up the amount then Tommy passed on the joke to the rest.

"My dad's paying for this," everyone said as they got their tea.

It was Old Bert's turn.

"I'll just have a cup of tea, love."

The young girl poured his tea.

"There you are, sir, that's eight pounds please."

All the lads watched as it kicked off.

"Eight pounds for a bloody cup of tea? You must be joking, I'm not paying it, you can take your tea back."

As the young girl tried to explain, Tommy went up and paid the bill with some of the money he had got from the Americans. Old Bert turned around and saw that he'd been had and, after a minute or two, saw the funny side.

Tommy's mother had packed plenty of snap for him and Barry,

including some pork pies and pasties, which Tommy handed around, making sure Old Bert had some. Norman's mum had packed him his favourite sandwiches; peanut butter with Bovril. Grizzly and Daft Dave had beef dripping on their sandwiches.

Once Old Bert had finished his tea, he went up to their Billy and warned him if he hit him one more time up the back end, he'd beat seven colours of shit out of him.

Tommy found Norman a bus with a shortwave radio and shouted to everyone to start making a move. They, along with Barry, had hatched a little plan for Hard Man Ray, to get him back for bullying Norman. The Americans asked if it was okay to ride with Elvis. The King of Rock and Roll obliged; he liked the attention you know.

The buses started up again and one by one followed Tommy up the road. Hard Man Ray was still unaware that dead Stanley was travelling with him. While Ray was in the café, Barry and Tommy had moved Stanley's body to the seat directly behind the driver's cab. Tommy had thought Old Stanley would have seen the funny side, especially as Hard Man Ray would always get on at Stanley while he was at the club, and in not a very nice way. No doubt, Ray would turn around sooner or later and see a dead body looking at him.

On the way back, Norman, Daft Dave, Kipper and Spanner kept overtaking each other and then 'Return to Sender' came on the radio. Elvis turned it up, to the delight of his American passengers; they all had a good sing-song.

The train of buses was putting a good few miles behind it when *bang*! It was the front right tyre of Digger's bus. Digger fought to control the vehicle, struggling with the wheel as the bus swerved from left to right. It looked as if he was about to go off the road, but it was the great strength of the man that held the steering wheel straight and kept the big bus stable on the road until it came to a halt. The others stopped behind, and Billy ran into the back of Bert one more time.

One of them called on the shortwave to Tommy at the front to stop, while Barry brought his vehicle up beside Digger's and changed the wheel. This knocked them back a good hour before they all got going again. Norman moved up the pack once more, taking every opportunity to overtake.

"Norman's got passengers on his bus again!" someone came on the radio and said.

Tommy called Norman on the radio and told him to stop and let them off, so he pulled up and did just that. Hard Man Ray thought it was funny and couldn't help himself having a jibe on the shortwave at Norman.

"Norman, you're such a knob."

"Don't you have any passengers, Ray? Over," Norman replied.

"No! Over," said Ray.

"Are you sure? Over," Norman teased.

Hard Man Ray turned to see a blue-faced Stanley looking and smiling right at him.

"*A aaggghhhh*! Norman, just you wait!"

Everyone who had a shortwave could hear, and found it quite amusing.

"Don't blame me, Ray, you were the one who commandeered my bus. Over.

Tommy was listening and joined the conversation.

"He's right, Ray, you did take his bus."

After that, spooky noises were heard over the radio. Ray was not happy, in fact he was crapping himself. Tommy asked Ray if having a dead body on his bus frightened him. He knew by the sound of his voice that it did, he also knew Ray would never admit to the fact and would carry on playing the hard man. Ray said on the radio that things like that didn't scare him, but, in truth, he was *shaking like a shitting dog*!

"*Ooooooh!*" came down the radio. I think it was Norman.

Ray stayed very quiet after that, the encounter had obviously disturbed him. About half an hour away from Mr McManus' yard, two buses broke down within about five minutes of each other. The first was Grizzly's, his clutch had gone.

Tommy switched Grizzly's bus for the one on the back of Big Bertha, so that sorted that. Next it was Billy's bus, his radiator had blown. This time, however, there were no spare buses with which to swap, so Barry got a tow rope out of Brenda and got Old Bert to tow Billy. While Tommy and Barry were fixing the tow rope, Bert went up to their Billy and punched him hard on the chin. Billy, as you can imagine, didn't see it coming and fell over, landing on his back. Bert stood over him wagging his finger. "One more time, Billy, run into the back of me one more time and you'll be pushing the daisies up in the cemetery!"

As they got going again they came off the Great North Road at Newark and headed for Sheffield. About an hour later, Elvis dropped his very satisfied passengers off in the centre of Sheffield as they drove through.

*

It was about eight o'clock and Rosie had been waiting in Mr McManus' yard for nearly two hours. Mr McManus and a couple of his men were also waiting, keeping the yard open, when they heard the sound of Big Bertha's horn about half a mile away.

"Here they come!"

12

McManus' Yard

The sun had not long set when Big Bertha approached Mr McManus' yard with her headlights on and her small, orange flashing light on top of her cab beaming through the darkness. She gave way to the oncoming traffic, before turning right into the yard, followed by the others. In a way it was sad to see these buses, which would have clocked up a good few hundred thousand miles, if not more than a million miles throughout their lifetime, finishing the last few yards of their life's journey. Mr McManus and his men were directing the buses as to where they were to park. They were doing a good job parking them nose to nose and side by side down the yard.

Bert came in towing their kid and as he stopped, Billy ran into him one last time. Norman loved it as he pulled in; he felt like he was one of the men. For him, he had completed a mammoth task driving a bus for the first time, all the way from London at his young age.

Rosie was out with her clipboard taking all the registration numbers. All the drivers were also asked to give her the engine serial numbers for the records.

Barry was the last in and soon unloaded his bus off the back of Brenda, then filled Big Bertha up for Mr McManus with what was left of the diesel, just as Tommy had instructed. He then parked Brenda on the road outside the yard, ready to take everyone back home.

Mr McManus was met by an old couple getting off Norman's

bus.

"*Tommy*!"

Tommy sorted the elderly couple out and took them to a bus stop not far outside the yard, so they could get back to wherever it was they were going.

"Mr McManus," shouted Norman, "have you lost a big wad of cash?"

"Why, have you found one?"

Mr McManus looked a little worried and started rattling around in his pockets.

"No," Norman replied, "but I've found a rubber band!"

Mr McManus set off after Norman, no doubt to give him a crack, but Norman was quick to run off to Rosie and give his engine number to her, but as he was doing so Tommy came in and grabbed him by the collar.

"That's the third lot of passengers you've picked up today!" he said, then gave him a crack on the back of the head on behalf of Mr McManus.

Rosie smiled at Norman over her clipboard and spoke only one word to him:

"*Pillock*!"

Barry, with the help of Daft Dave and Spanner, took what he could out of the buses, including the shortwave radios.

Once everyone was on Barry's bus, Tommy got on with Rosie and made Norman get up so she had a seat as Mr McManus saw them off. All the drivers were tired. Tommy could see it had been a bigger task for them than was originally thought and unless he paid them something, there would be no way he'd get them to go again if things ever worked out. He split the rest of the money he had got from the Americans and divided it among the men, who were all very thankful.

"Do *I* get anything?" asked Norman.

"No, shut up," said Tommy.

"But if it wasn't for me picking up those Americans, you wouldn't have got the money to pay anyone anyway."

Tommy shook his head and smiled; he knew from that moment Norman would go far, he was a smart lad with prospects.

Barry dropped Rosie off first at her home before dropping the rest off just in time for last orders at The Shaft. The big lad offered to drop Tommy off, but Tommy had said he would rather walk home from here and clear his head. Barry and Norman drove off, the rest entered the club with some beer money in their pockets and they were going to spend it!

13

Waiting for the Engines

Saturday morning in McCue's yard and the phone rang at nine o'clock.

"Tommy, phone!" Rosie shouted down.

"Oh, the phones are back on!" Norman said with a guilty look.

"Who is it?" asked Tommy as he entered the office.

"Mr McManus."

"Hello Mr McManus!" said Tommy.

"Hello Tommy, did you forget anything last night?"

"No?"

Tommy was trying to think.

"Your sandwich box perhaps," said Mr McManus "or a newspaper, or even a *dead body*!"

"*Bloody hell*!" Tommy exclaimed. "I'll be right over."

Tommy went straight over to Sheffield to sort it out. He called the coroner before he left and met him there. At McManus' yard, the coroner asked quite a lot of questions and, as always, Tommy, in serious situations was honest in the story he told. The coroner told Tommy and Mr McManus that he was happy with the situation, but they should think themselves lucky there wouldn't be an inquest. When he had gone, taking old Stanley with him, Mr McManus turned to Tommy and gave him the biggest bollocking he'd ever had.

"Now, piss off and I'll have the engines to you in the next couple of weeks."

Mr McManus wasn't the sort to hold grudges. Tommy didn't

blame him for being mad, he just wondered how he could have forgotten poor old Stanley.

*

By Tuesday the first lot of engines had arrived at Tommy's yard and that man came back and bought the Austin 10 - things were looking up.

The barber from next door came to see Tommy.

"Tommy, with the help of Cllr Bumsgrove, we have traced the source of the smell of urine and it's coming from your back stairs. Can you please sort it out?"

"No problem, I'll sort it out right now," Tommy told the barber. He shouted down to Big Barry and Norman in the yard. "Hoy! You two dirty buggers! Stop pissing down the chimney at the back of these stairs!"

"There we are," said Tommy to the barber as he showed him out, "never put off until tomorrow a job you can do today."

*

That afternoon Cllr Bumsgrove drove into the yard, parked at the entrance then marched to Tommy's office carrying another letter.

"Now what?" asked Tommy.

"There has been no reply to my last letter to you within the allotted timescale. Therefore, I hereby give you this notice for you to attend court in ten days time, where I envisage the magistrates will have you pack up your filthy business before it proliferates."

In the yard Barry was watching Norman backing up with the crane as they were stacking the engines.

"Keep coming, keep coming."

Barry's attention was diverted to Cllr Bumsgrove coming down the stairs, yelling at Tommy then *bang*! Norman hit Cllr Bumsgrove's car with the crane. Norman jumped out to see a big dent in the front wing. The councillor went potty.

"Don't look at me," said Norman to everyone. "*You* said keep coming!" he said to Barry.

Tommy gave Norman and Barry a look that told them they were a pair of tossers.

"I was distracted by your shouting," Barry said to the councillor.

"We'd fix it for you," said Tommy, "but we can't fit you in until next month and unfortunately we won't be here. It looks like your car will still drive, so bugger off would you."

Bumsgrove got into his car and drove off at speed as Barry and Norman started laughing.

"It's not funny, you two, that little bastard's going to close us down and you two will be out of a job. You pair of pillocks have just made matters worse."

The laughter stopped. For the first time Barry and Norman saw the pressure Tommy was under and the situation suddenly hit them. Tommy made his way back to the office and sat at his desk looking down and miserable.

"I'd like to see him get it, the horrible little man," Rosie said after the councillor had gone.

Tommy knew it was time to get that legal advice he had been advised to get. He rang the number Mr McManus had given him and made an appointment for the following morning.

*

The next morning, Tommy was going to drive to Sheffield, but as his flatback lorry was too dirty to get in with his suit on, he came into the yard and asked Barry where the Austin was.

"You sold it!"

Tommy caught the train into Sheffield. There he found Paradise Square, a group of brick-fronted terraced offices, mostly accommodated by solicitors or accountants. Tommy found the one he wanted. It had a royal blue painted door and a polished brass plaque on the office wall next to the door, which read:

Freader and Freader

Solicitors

He entered the building and walked up to a reception desk. Double checking the name on a piece of scrap paper he had brought with him, Tommy asked for Mr Freader.

"Which Mr Freader?" asked the lady on the desk.

Tommy didn't know, but explained that Mr McManus had sent him.

"Oh, that would be Mr Charles Freader, our senior partner. Please take a seat and I will let him know you're here."

Tommy sat down on a chair near the desk. The day's papers were on a table next to where he sat, but he felt a little intimidated by the place and chose not to touch anything. He just sat there on the edge of his seat.

After a couple of minutes a door to the reception area opened and a tall elderly man walked in and introduced himself to Tommy. Mr Freader had a little stoop and windswept grey hair. His light grey suit was tailored from fine cloth and his black shoes were polished to a military standard. He invited Tommy into his office and ordered two teas for himself and his new client. Tommy immediately felt at ease with Mr Freader, as he told him that his good friend, Mr McManus, had mentioned that Tommy was coming to see him and he had heard a lot about this up-and-coming young man. Tommy was a little taken aback by the comment. He never would have thought Mr McManus would ever speak highly of him.

Tommy seemed to get on with Mr Freader from the moment they met. He told him his problem with the planning permission, Cllr Bumsgrove and his forthcoming court appearance. The other problem Tommy had was that he couldn't afford to have any legal representation and would be obliged if Mr Freader could just find him a loophole.

"Well, you needn't worry about my fee today, Tommy. Mr McManus has called in one of his many favours this firm owes him. As for the loophole, I'll give it some thought, but I can make you no promises that I will be able to pull a rabbit out of a hat."

After Tommy left, the train journey back seemed a long one. He felt vulnerable. Perhaps naively he had expected the solicitor to sort his problem out there and then. What if there was no loophole - and no bloody rabbit?

*

The next few days passed quite quickly, as the engines kept coming. Barry was having to stack some of them on top of one another to make space in the yard.

Tommy had drafted a letter for Rosie to type on airmail paper. It read-

ALLAN FINLAY

McCue Exports
'To Faraway Places'
Stumble Street
Old Town
Yorkshire
Great Britain
Tel: 3044

Dear Sirs

We are a small firm of exporters and we currently have available 20 No. Gardener 5LX Diesel Engines, Serial Nos. 97,000-102,000 and 30 No. AEC 9.6L Engines. They were all manufactured between 1954-1955 and are in good running order.

The engines are available to you at the very good price of £200 per engine, plus shipping costs. We hope this is of interest to you and look forward to hearing from you in due course.

Yours faithfully,

Thomas McCue

THOMAS McCUE

Tommy handed Rosie a list of foreign addresses he had obtained sometime prior, from various British Embassies around the world.

"There must be over a hundred names and addresses!" Rosie said.

She knew, therefore, she would have to type each letter out individually many times, together with the envelopes. Norman came in and asked what she was doing. She told him she was typing the same letter out a hundred or so times.

"You know in the future," he said, "I bet someone invents a machine for offices where you can put just one letter in and then it takes a photo and copies it as many times as you want."

"Oh, shut up, Norman," she said as she set about the typing.

Each day after that she would take a handful of letters to the general post office just up the street and check each one was okay before posting.

*

Later on in that week it was Stanley's funeral, which was a burial following a short service at St Mary's Church. Although Tommy hadn't known Stanley that well, he felt it was only right that he attend, as Stanley died on his watch. Tommy went early to spend a little time at his dad's grave, before going into the church.

The funeral was a sad affair, in the fact that there were only about a dozen or so there, mostly from the club. The only one Tommy knew was Old Bert. He came into the church wearing a neck brace, noticed Tommy through his thick glasses and went to sit next to him. Tommy acknowledged him.

"All right, Bert? I thought for a moment you were the vicar. What's up with your neck?"

"Oh, Tommy, I had a great time last Friday, but I'm not taking our kid any more. His bus knocked me up the arse five or six times and now I've got whiplash to die for."

The church organ started up with a few wrong notes and then they brought Stanley's coffin in and placed it by the altar. The vicar got up to say a few words; words that honoured a hard working family man, who did a lot for charity. Bert leaned over to Tommy.

"I think I've come to the wrong funeral"

"You don't know how to whisper, do you, Bert?"

Stanley was then carried into the churchyard with the mourners following. Bert didn't see the six-foot deep hole in the ground and fell straight in.

"Are you all right, Bert?" Tommy enquired, trying not to laugh.

"I think I've broke m' blasted leg," said a voice from the grave.

The pallbearers put Stanley's coffin down to help. It took about twenty minutes before they could start to get Bert out because of the way he was placed and the fact that they had to secure his leg before he could be moved. Meanwhile, Tommy had run to a phone box and called an ambulance, which soon arrived for the first time in history - at a cemetery.

The pallbearers, with the help of a couple of the mourners, were just pulling Old Bert out of the grave as the ambulance men arrived, and they got straight to work.

"What's your name?"

"Lazarus!" someone shouted.

As Old Bert was carried by the pallbearers from the churchyard to the ambulance, two, scruffy snotty-nosed kids were at the church gates.

"I hope they at least make sure I'm dead before they try to bury me," said one to the other.

Bert was driven to the hospital so they could set his leg.

The grave was free and now it was Stanley's turn. That's where he was planted, in an unmarked grave at the edge of the churchyard. Buried and forgotten. Tommy was saddened by this, although he thought it might have been what Stanley wanted. The experience had just added to Tommy's desire to make something of himself, but with his appointment at the court just around the corner, it didn't look good.

14

In Court

The day Tommy had been dreading soon came along. Mr Freader hadn't phoned. Tommy had been chasing him the last couple of days, but to no avail. That morning Tommy went in his suit for an early breakfast at Kathy's. He didn't go because he was hungry, because he wasn't. He just needed to see Kathy, hopefully to get a little support.

"So, will you end up doing time?" Kathy teased as she served Tommy his breakfast.

"No, it's worse," he said, "I'll lose everything."

"Well, there's nothing you can do about it, so why worry?" she said. "Just take it on the chin and don't let that horrible lot get you down."

Tommy left the café feeling not much better and called at his yard on his way to court. The last load of engines had been delivered and the little yard was looking rather crammed.

The telephone rang. Rosie was busy typing, so Tommy answered it.

"McCue's."

"Tommy, it's Charles Freader. I'm sorry it's taken so long, but I believe I have found you a loophole."

*

The courtroom was full. Many from the council members had taken time off to see 'the fall of Tommy McCue'. Cllr Bumsgrove was seated in the middle with a big pile of files on his knees and a proud look on his face. Tommy was sitting in the dock sideways to the bench.

"All stand."

The chief magistrate, who had a taller back to his chair than the rest, was Cllr Pollock. He read:

"Thomas McCue, you are charged with trading on a site at Stumble Street without having planning permission. How do you plead?"

"Not guilty, chairman, sir," Tommy replied.

"Tommy, I'm not to be addressed as chairman unless it's in my club. In this court you will address me as 'Your Honour'. Now, do you have any representation?"

"No, Your Honour, I can't afford it."

Cllr Bumsgrove was called to the stand. Being the expert witness, he told the court that he had examined the records showing that Mr McCue had never ever applied for planning permission in his life.

"He is unequivocal, he is very perspicacious in promoting antidisestablishmentarianism." He went on to tell the court, "Under the rules of the council, no one is permitted to trade at a premise without having planning permission approved by the town's planning committee. Therefore, Your Honourable Worship, I recommend that Mr McCue is given a ten-day notice to cease trading on Stumble Street and move all his goods and storage off the site."

The chief magistrate looked at the other magistrates in the hope one had a dictionary, but dared not ask for help, as this might undermine his authority. The other magistrates were also in the same position. Tommy couldn't believe the venom and hatred of this guy, Cllr Bumsgrove was going beyond the call of duty. Tommy remembered the words of his solicitor, 'drag it out where you can for as long as you can, in order to mess them about'.

"Mr McCue," said the chief magistrate, "do you have anything to say?"

"Yes, Your Honour, what does antidisestablishmentarianism mean?"

"Never mind what that means!" said Pollock. "It's not the fault of this court that you don't understand big words. Now, have you anything else to say?"

"Cllr Pollock, I don't understand; sorry, Your Honourable Worship. Speaking breviloquently, nobody's ever objected before and I haven't built anything on site, so I don't see why I need planning permission and even if I did, the thousand pound planning fee seems a bit steep."

"You need planning permission for everything, especially a filthy business like yours. Now is there anything you would like to say before I pass judgement?"

"Just go through it one more time please, My Lord," Tommy replied.

"It's *Your Honour*!"

Pollock went through the details one more time as to why Tommy would have to close his yard.

"I still don't understand, sir, Your Honour, sir. You see, I took some legal advice before I came to court and as the law stands, I don't need planning permission because I have been trading on that site for more than five years and, therefore, this gives me 'Grandfather Rights'. The council's accusations would have been justified if they had brought the case to court within that first five-year period of me being there."

The court fell silent.

Cllr Bumsgrove stood up and shouted.

"You can't prove you have traded there for over five years! I implore the court to close Mr McCue's idiosyncratic business down immediately!"

Tommy put his hand in his pocket and pulled out some old invoices and delivery notes showing the address of his yard at Stumble Street - they were five and a half years old. The papers were passed to the bench.

"I'm afraid McCue has a case, we cannot ask him to vacate his yard. The Grandfather Rights stand," said one of the magistrates.

Pollock lifted his hammer, and before tapping it down onto its wooden base pronounced:

"Case dismissed."

Remembering again Mr Freader's advice, Tommy walked out of the courtroom gracious in his victory, but he couldn't help turning his head to glance at Cllr Bumsgrove sitting in the middle of his colleagues looking very angry and red-faced. Tommy just nodded and smiled to him as he made his way out.

*

On his way home Tommy passed The Fitzwilliam public house and after such a stressful day felt the urge for a pint. The small pub stood at the top of a steep street and Tommy passed it just about every day, but very rarely went in. As he entered he noticed Old Bert sitting at the bar with his leg in plaster and he was still wearing his neck brace.

"All right, Bert, how's the leg?"

"Oh, not too bad, Tommy. I have to keep the plaster on for a couple of months then it should be okay, but it's my neck that's giving me bother."

The landlady walked up to Tommy.

"I suppose you want a pint?"

"Please, if it's not too much trouble and can I pay one on for Bert?"

"He's had enough and we are closing soon, so hurry up and drink it," she said as she gave Tommy his pint.

"Nothing like service with a smile," said Bert.

The landlady gave him a funny look. Bert asked Tommy how he went on in court.

"Good,"

"I knew you would, lad," said Old Bert, smiling.

In the corner was Hard Man Ray drinking with a couple of his mates. Ray was still mad from the Stanley incident. He shouted over to Tommy.

"I didn't know they let bodysnatchers in here. How about I teach you a lesson about it, right here, right now?"

Ray's mates were loving it.

"Ignore the drunken bums, Tommy, they are out for a fight," said Bert, "and there's three of them, and I can't help you because my eyesight is not what it was and I've got a broken leg. Oh, and a bad neck."

Tommy looked at Bert.

"With all due respect, you silly old bugger, if there was nothing wrong with you, I don't think you would be much help."

Hard Man Ray came up to Tommy.

"I've never understood a man having a ponytail," said Old Bert.

"Why's that, Bert?" asked Tommy.

"Well, it's not the ponytail, it's what you find under a pony's tail that worries me."

Without warning, Ray threw a right punch at Tommy, which hit him on the cheek. Tommy didn't move.

"You punch like a child," he told Ray.

Ray started throwing punches at Tommy, who by now had his guard up, then Ray's two mates joined in the fight. Tommy started to fight back, but three of them were too much and he started to take a beating. The landlady was shouting her head off then Tommy hit one hard, nearly knocking his head off. One of Ray's mates then stood behind Tommy trying to hold his arms behind his back while the other two punched. Old Bert calmly watched then lifted up his walking stick and brought it down hard on top of the head of the one who was trying to hold Tommy. Ray's mate collapsed in pain. Tommy turned to Bert, who seemed very pleased with himself as he gave Tommy a nod.

With one man down, Ray's team started to suffer as Tommy laid into them until Ray's other mate ran out, leaving Ray on his own. Tommy got hold of him and gave him some more until he lay on the floor covered in blood with Tommy standing over him.

"You had better keep out of my way in future or next time you won't be getting up."

Ray got up, nodded defeat and left.

"Tommy McCue! You're barred!" cried the angry landlady.

"Why me? I didn't start it. Are you barring the other three?"

"No," she said.

"That's not fair," Old Bert chipped in. "Why's that?"

"Because they are my best customers and drink more beer than you do."

"Well, if you're barring Tommy, I'm barring myself you old witch," said Bert. "Come on, Tommy, there are better places to frequent."

The pair walked outside.

"Are you okay, Tommy?"

Tommy said he was, he had a bust lip, but otherwise he was fine.

"Did you see how I saved your life? Who's a silly old bugger now, eh?" Bert teased.

"Yes, it's a good job you have a broken leg or you might have killed them," Tommy said, then took Old Bert by the arm and helped him home.

On the way home Bert turned to Tommy.

"Do you remember all those years ago when I came to your school to tell you about your dad? Remember I said that you should make him proud? Well, just for the record, lad, I think he would be very proud of you. You remind me a lot of your dad, he was my best friend you know and I miss him dearly."

"I miss him too, Bert, and thank you," said Tommy.

"Thank me for what?"

"For being there. I know you have been watching over me since my dad died. You're the one who has been leaving the fish on our doorstep, aren't you?" Tommy asked.

Old Bert just smiled as they walked on to his street.

"Never mind the fish; remember I've just saved your life! Keep going as you're going, lad, you'll get there if you keep working as hard as you do. Goodnight, Tommy lad."

Off up the garden path he went.

"Bert! That's not your house it's next door's, you blind old bat!"

15
A Little Bit of Luck

It took poor old Rosie a couple of weeks to type all the letters. Tommy noticed her fingers had plasters on them due to the blisters she had from the constant typing. He had told her to leave the last few, but Rosie said that she only had about six more to do, and she battled on. Tommy knew he had a good one in Rosie.

"I hope you stay with me, Rosie, after I make it big."

"I'll have retired by then," she replied.

Once all the letters had gone, Tommy couldn't wait for the replies to come flooding in. However, as the weeks went by, nothing arrived. The engines just sat there in the yard getting covered in leaves and then blanketed in snow. The whole job seemed to have slowed down, the shelter sheets were becoming harder to find and by the spring, things had become dire.

The council had gone quiet too; they were leaving Tommy alone for the time being anyway. Rosie had cut her hours down to just half a day a week to help Tommy out and Barry was working at a garage out of town on Saturdays to help make up his wage.

*

Tommy decided to go to Kathy's Café. On the way there he walked down Spring Lane and as he passed a bank that ran down to a small field he noticed two familiar faces. Little Harry and Eddie were standing on the bank and some older boys were throwing their shoes, with some force, at the two little lads. Both Harry and Eddie were endeavouring to fight back, hurling the shoes back at the older boys, but not hard enough to hurt them. Harry and Eddie were outnumbered and outmatched, but they were brave enough to hold back their tears, then little Eddie saw someone he knew.

"Uncle Tommy! *Help!*" he shouted as he got a shoe thrown into his ribs.

Tommy looked at the two of them.

"I can't just step in like that; you've got to learn to fight your own battles."

Tommy ducked to escape an incoming shoe.

"You start and I'll tell m' dad, you big bully," said one of the older lads to Tommy.

"I think you lot are the bullies in this case," Tommy replied.

"We can't fight, we're no strong enough," said Harry as he tried to lob a shoe back.

"Well, if you're not strong enough, you need to use your brains, it's up here for thinking, down there for dancing."

"Tha' what? What good will that do?" Harry asked.

"Well, whose shoes are they?"

"They're theirs," Eddie shouted.

"So, don't throw the shoes back to them, throw them as far into those hawthorn bushes as you can," Tommy said.

Harry and Eddie did just that and the other boys started to shout and cry as they ran barefooted into the hawthorns after their shoes - the battle was won.

"Now bugger off you two before they find them and remember, there's no such word as *can't!*" Tommy shouted.

"Thanks, Uncle Tommy!" they yelled as they ran away.

Tommy carried on down the lane and headed for the café.

"Can I just have a couple of boiled eggs, please Kathy?" he

asked as he entered.

"Why *boiled* eggs?"

"Oh, I just fancy something different,"

"You're skint, aren't you?"

He smiled and lied. He admired the fact that Kathy was smarter than she made out, and then she brought him a Full Monty anyway.

"It's okay, Tommy, this one's on the house," she said.

"I might just take you for another walk in the park," he said.

"Why the park?"

"It's free!"

*

It was a warm morning and Tommy was sitting on the stairs that led to his office. With his hands on his chin, he was deep in thought, looking at the engines in his yard and a sorry-looking Brenda parked in the corner. They were taking up room and Tommy had started to think it was about time he did something about it. The only thing there was to do was to scrap them, even if the scrap value was only a fraction of their worth as second-hand engines.

He pondered the decision for quite a while then stood up and started up the stairs to the office where he would phone Mr McManus to come and collect them. As he went up the stairs his head was low; he felt he had failed, all this trouble for nothing. Well, at least, he thought he'd tried his best.

"Tommy!" shouted the postman. "I've got your post; more bills no doubt!"

"Yep," Tommy said with a put-on smile as he went back down to take the post.

He thanked the postman and walked back upstairs alone to his office, where he put the post down on his desk and picked up the telephone to phone Mr McManus. As he dialled the number, Tommy looked at the post. He noticed that one of the letters was marked 'Airmail', so he put the phone down. The stamp showed it was from Hong Kong.

He took his letter opener and carefully ran it across the envelope, and inside were a couple of pages of lightweight airmail paper. He pulled the letter out of its envelope and sat down at his desk. The letter read:

YU CHAN LI SHIPPING
Machinery Imports
Kowloon Bay
Hong Kong

Dear Mr McCue

Wiv refewrence at you letter offewing the sale of the engine. We would like to order from you 10 Nos. (TEN) AEC engines and agwee your asking price of £200.00 pre unit.

Our bank details are attached for your own bank to set up a letter of credit. Once we receive delivery of these first 10 Nos. engines, we would like to order 10 Nos. engines every month after that. Please let us know if you can supry our demonds.

Please awange with our shitting agent (details attached) for you to deliver engines to Liverpool Port.

We look forward to dealing wiv you, Mr McCue. We hope our business relationship is long, prosperous and honourable.

Assuring you the best at all times.

Kindest wishes,

HARRY CHAN

HARRY CHAN.

Tommy seemed frozen; he read the letter again.

*

Tommy contacted Mr Chan's shipping agent in Liverpool and arranged for the export of the first ten. He then ran up to the bank where his bank manager set up the letter of credit.

*

Tommy and Barry put each engine into a wooden crate and nailed the top down. They loaded up Tommy's small clapped-out lorry he used for collecting shelter sheets, with ten engines, using the old Coles crane. When they had finished they roped the crates down. The poor little lorry didn't look like it could hold any more, nevertheless, it was there all ready to go the following day, it's cargo about to journey to the other side of the world.

The engines were booked onto a cargo ship that was to set sail from Liverpool at twelve noon the next day. Tommy had to get them there before ten.

*

By seven the next morning; Tommy was heading over The Pennines, the backbone of England. He was making good time, but the Manchester traffic had slowed him down on his way to Liverpool.

Quarter to ten and he was in Liverpool panicking, looking for the docks. When he finally found them, he started down the road to the cargo area. At the gates to the docks a policeman was walking up the road and he waved Tommy to stop.

"You are trailing oil all over the road. You will have to stop and leave the vehicle here, you can't go any farther," the policeman said, reaching for his notebook. "You look overloaded, your tyres look illegally bald and I bet you can't surprise me by telling me you have any insurance."

Tommy could see the ship berthed on the dock; so near yet so far. He put his head in his hands.

"Bollocks!"

No, I've got this far, I'm not giving up now, he thought. *There's no such word as can't!*

"Officer, I'm very sorry, but I beg you, sir, please allow me to get these engines onto that ship. A lot of people are depending on me, therefore, sir, I appeal to your good nature and I apologise for the oil. I promise you it won't happen again."

Everyone likes a trier, especially an honest one. The policeman let him through. With a minute to spare, Tommy delivered the engines and they were soon loaded onto the ship.

He then drove to a spot in the sun where he could watch the ship start her long journey. He parked up his lorry and with the westerly sea breeze coming in from offshore, he got out and sat down on a large grass bank overlooking the sea. After a couple of hours the ship plotted a course for Hong Kong and set sail. Tommy watched from the coast as she sailed by and out of sight. A great feeling of achievement came over him. He hoped then and there that this shipment was the first of many, and maybe, just maybe, this was the beginning of something great.

Epilogue

Tommy McCue sold his yard on Stumble Street and moved to a much larger one on the outskirts of the town. Over the next thirty years the little business went from strength to strength, exporting several forty-foot containers every week with as many as twenty-four engines per container. Other container loads of vehicle parts such as propshafts, gearboxes, axles and lorry cabs were also sold. Open-top buses to America, old single-deckers to Mauritius and second-hand lorries to Egypt, Taiwan, Africa and many other faraway places.

Tommy became good friends with his first customer, Mr Chan. They made each other rich men and their business relationship was indeed honourable and long lasting.

Mr Chan sold the engines into China where they were bought mainly by the Chinese fishermen for their boats, and it wasn't long before most of the famous junk boats in Hong Kong harbour had Tommy's old second-hand bus engines installed. With sometimes over a million miles on them, the engines still to this day, reliably chug away quite happily in their Far East retirement.

*

Barry stayed loyal to Tommy and continued to work for him for many years. Norman got into photocopiers in the seventies and computers in the eighties and, as Tommy thought, he became a millionaire in his own right.

Tommy continued to deal with old Mr McManus and after the old man retired, Tommy kept a watchful eye on him and made sure he was well cared for, along with Old Bert, whose leg mended. but his neck was never the same. Old Bert and Mr McManus became good friends in their old age; the pair were regulars at the local greyhound track, where Mr McManus usually had a dog running.

Little Harry and Eddie ended up working for Tommy after they left school. He made sure they didn't go without. Grizzly started dealing in engines and did quite well for himself selling mainly to Tommy.

Tommy and Barry asked Hard Man Ray if he would go to Ireland to collect a bus in the late sixties, but there was no bus to pick up. They gave him a false address and his ferry money. It was all just a big joke, but the funny thing was, they have never seen or heard from him since.

Spanner now works for a local tyre company and occasionally brings a bus back for Tommy when he can. He still drinks in the club on a Saturday night at the same table with Kipper.

Kipper's pigeons never came home; he waited for weeks. However, his birds found a new home in Trafalgar Square, where they multiplied and have now become a national attraction. Kipper still visits them whenever he can.

Cllr Bumsgrove moved to work for another council not long after the court case; nobody knew if he jumped or was pushed.

Rosie retired not long after Tommy moved yards, and Kathy, would you believe it, married Daft Dave, but it didn't last long. She had no luck when it came to men, but she still serves the best breakfast in town. There is usually a Rolls Royce parked outside her café at about ten o'clock each morning. Apparently it belongs to a chap who used to go years ago for his breakfast, when he had nowt!

Printed in Great Britain
by Amazon

45773271R00076